Celebrate . . . the Word

David Adam
Gary Chapman
David E. Flavell
Tim LaHaye and Jerry B. Jenkins
Hilary McDowell
Josh McDowell
Stormie Omartian
Rob Parsons
Frank Peretti
Nigel D. Pollock
Vaughan Roberts
John Stott
Philip Yancey

British Library Cataloguing in Publication Data
A catalogue record for this book is available from the British Library
ISBN 1-900836-6-8

Typeset by WestKey Ltd, Falmouth, Cornwall
Printed by Ebner, Ulm

Contents

Foreword

'Lord make us one, but not the same' is the marvellous title of a book by Joel Edwards who is the head of the Evangelical Alliance. How true! Life would be so dull if we were all clones of one another. It is important that we celebrate our differences rather than resent or criticise them.

We all have different tastes in music, clothes, furnishings, food and of course books and writers. There are some authors whose books grip me from page one and I lose all track of time and its pressure in order to devour the pages. Others I find a struggle to understand, perhaps because 'being a bear of little brain' I find them too intellectual to comprehend!

I was therefore thrilled to discover 'Celebrate the Word' which offers the reader extracts from different Christian writers... a veritable feast of appetizers to whet the appetite for the whole banquet. Here is a lovely selection to encourage us to get to know the writers' styles and decide for ourselves if we would enjoy reading more of their work.

I already have Rob Parsons' new book 'The Sixty Minute Mother' on my list! Having read all his previous books, I know I will enjoy it. He is a compelling and sometimes hilarious speaker who writes as he speaks, and tells us the truth without making us feel like utter failures. Thank you Rob.

And ...too late... I already have a copy of the New Living Translation and it's wonderful. I have always loved the Living Bible and the 'TouchPoint Bible' (using the New Living Translation) is definitely my favourite version to date.

There is so much variety in 'Celebrate the Word' that there is bound to be something to suit all tastes, to strengthen, equip and encourage us as we seek to become mature in the Christian life. We need all the help we can get.

I heartily recommend it and hope you'll be inspired through it to increase your library.

Fiona Castle

Preface

'A book is for all year round, not just World Book Day.'
                                   Nina Bawden, children's author

World Book Day 2000 is a wonderful opportunity to acknowledge the benefits we can all derive from the printed word. Even in an age of increasing technological advance, books still have a key part to play in our education, our leisure and our understanding of the world in which we live. For the Christian, God's Word the Bible is a vital ingredient.

'Celebrate the Word' showcases a fine collection of best selling Christian writers. Extracts from their works reveal creativity, wisdom, knowledge and humour. From family values to student relationships, issues of current debate and ancient enquiry, real and imagined events, and the certainty of God's Word, each book represented answers a need. Is it yours?

This celebration specially compiled for World Book Day 2000 provides the reader with an insight into the style and passions of each author. Stott, Yancey, McDowell, Parsons are just some of the talented writers in this diverse collection which aims to stimulate thought, encouragement and debate.

Our thanks go to all the authors and publishers who have willingly shared their thoughts with us.

A familiar book can bring comfort. A new book can bring surprises. May your coming year be filled with many good books and may the pages rise up to greet you.

The Visitation

Frank Peretti

Nothing interesting ever happened in the small town of Antioch until now. Without warning Antioch has suddenly become a gateway for the supernatural – from sightings of angels and messianic images materialising in the sky to a weeping crucifix with the power to heal.

Then a mysterious self-proclaimed prophet appears with a message…but is it from God?

The startling secret behind this visitation ultimately pushes one man into a confrontation that will forever alter the lives of everyone involved.

Frank Peretti is without doubt the undisputed master of supernatural thrillers. This latest struggle between the forces of good and evil will have your heart pounding and the pages turning long into the night.

Word Publishing
ISBN: 0-8499-1179-6

Price: £14.99

Copyright © 1999 Frank Peretti

First published in 1999 by Word Publishing
Nashville, Tennessee

Prologue

The hammer rang against the nail, piercing skin, cutting vessels. It rang against the nail, piercing muscle, chipping bone. It rang against the nail, anchoring arm to rough-hewn wood. It rang. It rang. It rang.

And then the ringing stopped, and the young man hung there under the scorching sun, faint with pain, alone. He could not shift his weight, flex his knees, or even turn his head without feeling the fire of the nails. His wrists were swelling around the nail heads. His blood was drying in the sun, turning brown on the wood.

He cried out, but God did not listen. It could have been God who drove the nails, then put his hammer down and turned away, smiling in victory. It could have been God who left him to bake and bleed in the sun, unable to stand, unable to fall, as the sun marked the passing hours across the cloudless sky.

Stinking with sweat. Crimson with sunburn. Dried blood crackling around the nails. Pain the only reality.

He cried out, but in the cauldron of his sun-boiled mind he heard only the voices of his accusers and the ringing, ringing, ringing of the hammer – sounds that would forever haunt his memory and echo through his nightmares.

'You're a child of the devil,' they said. A child of the devil who needed to be contained.

A child of the devil?

He cried out once again, and this time, a voice, a mind, answered and a power coursed through him. Suddenly, he could bear the pain and make it fuel for his will. With burning will, he determined he would live.

And living, he knew what he would do.

1

Sally Fordyce left the house as soon as the breakfast dishes were done, walking a little, jogging a little along Highway 9 – a narrow, straight-as-a-string two-lane with a fading white line and an evenly spaced parade of utility poles. This was eastern Washington State, quiet and solitary. Wheat fields, spring green, stretched in every direction over the prairie swells. Straight ahead, the highway dipped and rose gently into the distance until it narrowed to a vanishing point at the far horizon. The sun was warm, the breeze a little biting. It was April.

Sally was nineteen, blonde, slightly overweight, and severely unhappy, mainly because she was no longer married. She had believed everything Joey, the trucker, told her about love, and how she was that girl silhouetted on his mud flaps. The marriage – if it happened at all – lasted three months. When he found another woman more 'intellectually stimulating,' Sally was bumped from the truck's sleeper and found herself coming full circle, right back to being Charlie and Meg's daughter living at home again. She had to keep her room clean, help with dinner and dishes, get home by eleven, and attend the Methodist church with them every Sunday. Again, her life was not her life.

She had tasted freedom, she thought, but she was turned away. She had no wings to fly and nowhere to fly even if she did. Life wasn't fair. (To hear Charlie tell it, he and Meg must have made up a list of all the dumb mistakes they hoped she would never make and given her a copy. Needless to say, things were tense.)

Even before she tried Joey, the trucker, Sally used to find escape out on the wheat prairie in the stillness of the morning. Now she returned, even fled to this place. Out here, she heard no voice but her own thoughts, and her thoughts could say whatever they wanted. She could pray too, sometimes aloud, knowing no one but God would hear her. 'Dear God, please don't leave me stuck here. If you're there, send a miracle. Get me out of this mess.'

In all fairness, it was past time for Sally to feel that way. Except for those who had wheat farming in their blood and couldn't wait to climb on a combine, most everyone growing up in Antioch heard a call from elsewhere – *anywhere* – sooner or later. When they came of age, all the kids who could find a way out left – usually – for good. Sally had come of age, all right, but had not found a way out. Charlie and Meg would probably tell you that she was not the kind to look for one, either. She was still waiting for it to come to her.

The halfway point of her jog was a spreading cottonwood at the top of a shallow rise, the only tree in sight. It was monstrous, and had to have been growing there long before the roads, farms, or settlers came along. Sally double-timed her way up the rise and was breathing hard by the time she reached it. She'd developed a routine: Every day she braced herself against the huge trunk and stretched out her leg muscles, then sat and rested for a moment between two prominent roots on the south side. Recently, a short prayer for a miracle had also become part of the routine.

The stretches went easily enough. She had cooled down, her breathing had settled, she could feel the flush in her cheeks from the exercise and the cool air.

She rounded the tree –

And almost jumped out of her skin.

A man was sitting between the two roots, exactly in her spot, his back against the gnarled trunk and his wrists draped lazily over his knees. He had to have been there all during her stretching-out, and she was immediately curious, if not offended, that he had said or done nothing to indicate his presence.

'Oh!' she gasped, then caught her breath. 'Hello. I didn't see you there.'

He only chuckled and smiled at her with a kindly gaze. He was a remarkably handsome man, with olive skin, deep brown eyes, and tightly curled black hair. He was young, perhaps as young as she was. 'Good morning, Sally. Sorry if I startled you.'

She probed her memory. 'Have we met before?'

He shook his head teasingly. 'No.'

'Well, who are you?'

'I'm here to bring you a message. Your prayers have been heard, Sally. Your answer is on his way. Be looking for him.'

She looked away for only a moment, just a slight, eye-rolling gesture of consternation. 'Be looking for who –?'

He was gone.

'Hey!'

She walked around the cottonwood, looked up and down the road and across every field, and even looked straight up the trunk of the tree.

He was gone, just like that, as if he'd never been there.

After one more hurried trip around the tree, she stopped, a hand against the trunk to steady herself, her eyes scanning the prairie. Her heart was beating faster than when she'd come up the rise. Her breathing was rapid and shallow. She was shaking.

At Our Lady of the fields church in Antioch, Arnold Kowalski was busy dust-mopping the quaint little sanctuary, pushing the wide broom between the pews and down the center aisle, moving a little slowly but doing a thorough job. Arnold had been a soldier, a carpenter, a diesel mechanic, and a mail carrier, and now, since retiring, he had taken upon himself the unofficial title of church custodian. It wasn't a paid position, although the church did provide a little monetary gift for him each month as an expression of love and gratitude. He just did it for God, a few hours a few days a week, pure and simple. It brought him joy, and besides, he liked being in this place.

He'd been a devout member of Our Lady of the Fields for some forty years now. He never missed Sunday morning mass if he could help it. He never failed to make it to confession, though now at seventy-two the confessions were getting shorter and the penance easier. He liked to think that God was happy with him. He considered himself happy enough with God.

Except for one thing, one minor grief he had to carry as he moved slowly down the center aisle pushing his broom. He couldn't help wishing that God would pay just a little attention to Arnold's arthritis. It used to flare up occasionally; now it was only on occasion that it didn't. He was ashamed to think such a thought, but he kept thinking it anyway: *Here I am serving God, but God keeps letting it hurt.*

His hands throbbed, his feet ached. His knuckles cried out no matter which way he gripped the broom. He was never one to complain, but today, he almost felt like crying.

Maybe I'm not serving God enough, he thought. *Maybe I need to work longer. Maybe if I didn't take any money for what I do here . . .*

What am I missing? he wondered. *What am I leaving out?*

He always took off his hat when he entered the building and blessed himself before entering the sanctuary. Right now, as usual, he was wearing his blue coveralls. Perhaps a tie would show more respect.

He pushed a little more dust and dirt down the center aisle until he stepped into a beam of sunlight coming through a stained-glass window. The sun felt warm on his back and brought him comfort, as if it were God's hand resting on his shoulders. From this spot he could look up at the carved wooden crucifix hanging above the altar. He caught the gaze of the crucified Christ.

'I don't want to complain,' he said. Already he felt he was over-stepping his bounds. 'But what harm would it do? What difference would it make to this big wide world if one little man didn't have so much pain?' It occurred to Arnold that he had addressed God in anger. Ashamed, he looked away from those gazing wooden eyes. But the eyes drew him back, and for a strange, illusory moment they seemed alive, mildly scolding, but mostly showing compassion as a father would show to a child with a scraped knee. Sunlight from another window brought out a tiny sparkle in the corners of the eyes, and Arnold had to smile. He could almost imagine those eyes were alive and wet with tears.

The sparkle grew, spreading from the corners of the eyes and reaching along the lower eyelids.

Arnold looked closer. Where was the light coming from that could produce such an effect? He looked above and to the right. It had to be coming through that row of small windows near the ceiling. To think he'd been attending this church for so many years and never noticed this before. It looked just as if –

A tear rose over the edge of the eyelid and dropped onto the wooden cheek, tracing a thin wet trail down the face and onto the beard.

Arnold stared, frozen, his mind stuck between seeing and believing. He felt no sense of awe, no overshadowing spiritual presence. He heard no angelic choir singing in the background. All he knew was that he was watching a wooden image shed tears as he stood there dumbly.

Then his first coherent thought finally came to him. *I have to get up there.* Yes, that was the thing to do; that would settle it. He hurried as fast as the pain in his feet would allow him and brought a ladder from the storeroom in back. Pausing before the altar to bless himself, he stepped around the altar and carefully leaned the ladder against the wall. Every climbing step brought a sharp complaint from his feet, but he gritted his teeth, grimaced, and willed himself up the ladder until he came eye to eye, level to level with the carved face.

His eyes had not been playing tricks on him. The face, only a third life-sized, was wet. He looked above to see if there was a leak in the ceiling but saw no sign of a device or some kind of trickery. Nothing.

He reached, then hesitated from the very first tinge of fear. Just what was he about to touch? *Dear God, don't hurt me.* He reached again, shakily extending his hand until his fingertips brushed across the wet trail of the tears.

He felt a tingling, like electricity, and jerked his hand

away with a start. It wasn't painful, but it scared him, and his hand began to quiver. Electric sensations shot up his arm like countless little bees swarming in his veins. He let out a quiet little yelp, then gasped, then yelped again as the sensation flowed across his shoulders, around his neck, down his spine. He grabbed the ladder and held it tightly, afraid he would topple off.

A strong grip.

A grip without pain. He stared at his hand. The vibration buzzed, and swirled under his skin, through his knuckles, across his palms, through his wrists. He lightened his grip, tightened it again, held on with one hand while he opened and closed the other, wiggling and flexing the fingers.

The pain was gone. His hands were strong.

The current rushed down his legs, making his nerves tingle and his muscles twitch. He hugged the ladder, his hands glued to the rungs, a cry bouncing off the wall only inches from his nose. He was shaking, afraid he would fall. He cried out, gasped, trembled, cried out again.

The electricity, the sensation – whatever it was – enveloped his feet and his scream echoed through the building.

Sunday, Pastor Kyle Sherman prayed the prayer of benediction, the pianist and organist began playing the postlude – a modern rendition of 'Be Still My Soul' – and the congregation of the Antioch Pentecostal Mission rose to leave. The after-service shuffling was the same as one would see in any church. Folks gathered up their coats, Bibles, Sunday school papers, and children, then formed slow-moving clusters in the aisles and doorways to joke and chat. Families, singles, friends, and visitors passed through the main doorway where the young pastor stood to shake their hands and greet them. Kids went as wild as their parents would tolerate, running outside after being scolded for running inside.

Dee Baylor was among the departing saints that day. A steady and constant presence at Antioch Mission, she was a robust, heavy-set woman in her forties with a prominent nose and hair that added measurably to her height. Short, mousy Blanche Davis and tightly permed, blue-rinsed Adrian Folsom were walking with her across the gravel parking lot as the three worked excitedly to keep the Christian grapevine alive.

'That's all he said?' Adrian asked.

Dee didn't mind repeating the story or any part of it. 'Just that "her answer was on his way." And according to Sally he said *his* way, not *its* way.'

'So who was he talking about?' asked Blanche.

'Maybe her future husband,' Adrian ventured. 'God told me I was going to marry Roger.'

'So what about the crucifix at the Catholic church?' Blanche wondered.

'You can't limit God,' Dee answered.

'No, you can't limit God,' Adrian agreed with extra insistence in her voice.

'But a weeping statue?' Blanche asked, making a crinkled face. 'That sounds awfully Catholic to me.'

'Well, it's something a Catholic would understand.'

Blanche considered that in silence.

'We need to be seeking the Lord,' said Dee, her eyes closing prayerfully. 'We need to be expecting. God has plans for Antioch. I think the Lord is ready to pour out his Spirit on this town.'

'Amen.' That was what Blanche wanted to hear.

'Amen,' Adrian echoed.

Dee looked up at the sky as if looking toward heaven. The clouds were breaking up now. Patches of blue were beginning to show, promising a pleasant afternoon.

Adrian and Blanche walked and continued the conversation until they noticed they were by themselves. They looked back.

'Dee?'

She was standing still, clutching her Bible to her bosom and looking heavenward, her lips moving rapidly as she whispered in another language.

'Dee?'

They hurried to her side. 'What is it?'

All she could do was point, then gasp, her hand over her mouth.

Adrian and Blanche looked quickly, afraid something might fall on them. They saw nothing but billowing clouds and patches of blue sky.

'I see Jesus,' Dee said in a hushed voice. Then, raising one hand toward the sky she shouted ecstatically, 'Jesus! I see you, I see you!'

Brother Norheim walked by. He was old, bent, and hard of hearing, but a respected church pillar. He knew how a church should be run and how the Spirit moved and how to properly wash out the communion cups so as not to offend the Lord. When he started 'Bless the Lord, O My Soul' from his pew in the evening service, everybody sang right along whether Linda Sherman could find the right key on the piano or not. He could see the ladies were excited about something.

'What are you looking at?'

'I see the Lord!' Dee gasped, and then she broke into a song. 'I see the Lord . . . I see the Lord . . . He is high and lifted up, and his train fills the temple!'

Adrian and Blanche kept staring at the clouds, hoping to spot something, making quick sideways glances at each other for clues.

Brother Norheim looked the sky over, smiling with three golden teeth and three gaps. 'The firmament showeth his handiwork!'

'What do you see?' Adrian finally asked.

Dee pointed. 'Don't you see him? Right there! He's looking right at us!'

Adrian and Blanche looked carefully, following the point of Dee's finger. Finally, Blanche drew in a slow, awe-struck gasp. 'Yeeesssss . . . Yes, I see him! I see him!'

'Where?' Adrian cried. 'I don't see him.'

'Isn't that incredible!'

Adrian put her head right next to Blanche's, hoping to gain the same perspective. 'Show me.'

Blanche pointed. 'See? There's the top of his head, and there's his ear and his beard . . .'

Adrian let out a crowlike squawk she usually saved for funny jokes and deep revelations. 'AWWW! You're right! You're right!'

Now all three women were pointing and looking while Dee kept singing in and out of English. Brother Norheim moved on, glad to see the saints on fire, but others came alongside to see what the commotion was all about. Dave White, the contractor, saw the face right away, but his wife, Michelle, never did. Adrian's husband, Roger, saw the face, but found it an amusing coincidence and nothing more. Don and Melinda Forester, a new couple in church, both saw the face but disagreed on which direction it was looking. Their kids, Tony and Pammie, ages eight and six, saw Jesus but also saw several different animals on top of his head.

'Look!' said Adrian. 'He's holding a dove in his hand, you see that?'

'Yeeahhhhh . . .' Dave White said in a hushed voice, his face filled with awe.

'He's ready to pour out his Spirit!' Dee announced with a prophetic waver in her voice.

'Eh, beats me,' said Roger, squinting at the sky.

'He's speaking to us in these last days!'

'You're crazy,' Michelle insisted. 'I don't see anything.'

'Hey Pastor Sherman!' Tony yelled. 'We see Jesus in the clouds!'

'There's a rooster!' Pammie squealed.

'It just kept going from there,' Kyle Sherman told me.

'The three women started seeing all kinds of things because the clouds kept changing. For a while Jesus had a dove in his hand, and then after that he turned into a door – you know, the door to the sheepfold, the door to heaven, whatever you want – and then –' Kyle looked toward the ceiling as he recalled the appearance of the sky. 'Uh . . . a flame, I think.' He drew it in the air with his hand. 'Kind of wavy, you know, up and down like a pillar of fire.'

Kyle hadn't used any names up to this point, so I asked him, 'Are you talking about Dee Baylor?'

He nodded, looking abashed.

'Adrian Folsom and Blanche Davis?'

Kyle nodded again, a reluctant yes.

'Makes sense,' I said, picking up my coffee cup and taking another swallow.

It was Monday, the typical pastor's day off. Kyle Sherman and I were sitting at my kitchen table with coffee cups and a bag of Oreo cookies between us. He was still in his twenties, dark-haired, wiry, a fresh horse ready to gallop.

For the past four months, he'd been at this table in this little house several times, keeping in touch and trying to be a good shepherd.

Life Application Study Bible

New Living Translation

How many times have you read your Bible and asked 'How can this possibly apply to my life?'

Many Christians do not read the Bible regularly. Why? Because they cannot find a connection between the timeless principles of Scripture and the everyday problems of life. If this has been your experience, then *The Life Application Study Bible* has been developed to help you.

God urges us to apply his Word, not just accumulated Bible knowledge. *The Life Application Study Bible* shows how to put into practice what we have learned. Its notes also explain difficult passages and give background information about Bible life and times.

The New Living Translation is accurate, easy to read, and excellent to study.

Tyndale House Publishers
ISBN: 0-8423-3267-7

Price: £27.99

Life Application Study Bible

New Living Translation

- Over 10,000 **Life Application Notes** help explain God's Word and challenge you to apply its truth to your life.
- **Personality Profiles** highlight significant people in the Bible and the lessons you can learn from their lives.
- **Book Introductions** include timelines, overviews, and outlines to help you understand and respond to each book's message.
- **Megathemes** explain the major theme of each book and their importance for you today.
- **Charts and Maps** are found throughout the text to help you quickly locate key places and grasp difficult concepts.
- **Index/Dictionary/Concordance** helps you quickly find the information you need for study and instruction.
- **Daily Reading Plan** provides an outline for reading the entire Bible in one year.

Acts

The Promise of the Holy Spirit

1 Dear Theophilus:
In my first book* I told you about everything Jesus began to do and teach ²until the day he ascended to heaven after giving his chosen apostles further instructions from the Holy Spirit. ³During the forty days after his crucifixion, he appeared to the apostles from time to time and proved to them in many ways that he was actually alive. On these occasions he talked to them about the Kingdom of God.

⁴In one of these meetings as he was eating a meal with them, he told them, 'Do not leave Jerusalem until the Father sends you what he promised. Remember, I have told you about this before. ⁵John baptized with* water, but in just a few days you will be baptized with the Holy Spirit.'

The Ascension of Jesus

⁶When the apostles were with Jesus, they kept asking him, 'Lord, are you going to free Israel now and restore our kingdom?'

⁷'The Father sets those dates,' he replied, 'and they are not for you to know. ⁸But when the Holy Spirit has come upon you, you will receive power and will tell people about

---

¹·¹   The reference is to the book of Luke.
¹·⁵   Or *in*; also in 1:5b.

me everywhere – in Jerusalem, throughout Judea, in Samaria, and to the ends of the earth.'

⁹It was not long after he said this that he was taken up into the sky while they were watching, and he disappeared into a cloud. ¹⁰ As they were straining their eyes to see him, two white-robed men suddenly stood there among them. ¹¹They said, 'Men of Galilee, why are you standing here staring at the sky? Jesus has been taken away from you into heaven. And someday, just as you saw him go, he will return!'

Matthias Replaces Judas

¹²The apostles were at the Mount of Olives when this happened, so they walked the half mile* back to Jerusalem. ¹³Then they went to the upstairs room of the house where they were staying. Here is the list of those who were present:

Peter,
John,
James,
Andrew,
Philip,
Thomas,
Bartholomew,
Matthew,
James (son of Alphaeus),
Simon (the Zealot),
and Judas (son of James).

1:12 Greek *a Sabbath day's journey*.

[14]They all met together continually for prayer, along with Mary the mother of Jesus, several other women, and the brothers of Jesus.

[15]During this time, on a day when about 120 believers★ were present, Peter stood up and addressed them as follows:

[16]'Brothers, it was necessary for the Scriptures to be fulfilled concerning Judas, who guided the Temple police to arrest Jesus. This was predicted long ago by the Holy Spirit, speaking through King David. [17]Judas was one of us, chosen to share in the ministry with us.'

[18](Judas bought a field with the money he received for his treachery, and falling there, he burst open, spilling out his intestines. [19]The news of his death spread rapidly among all the people of Jerusalem, and they gave the place the Aramaic name Akeldama, which means 'Field of Blood.')

[20]Peter continued, 'This was predicted in the book of Psalms, where it says, "Let his home become desolate, with no one living in it." And again, "Let his position be given to someone else." '★

[21]'So now we must choose another man to take Judas's place. It must be someone who has been with us all the time that we were with the Lord Jesus – [22]from the time he was baptized by John until the day he was taken from us into heaven. Whoever is chosen will join us as a witness of Jesus' resurrection.'

[23]So they nominated two men: Joseph called Barsabbas (also known as Justus) and Matthias. [24]Then they all prayed for the right man to be chosen. 'O Lord,' they said, 'you know every heart. Show us which of these men you have

---

1:15 Greek *brothers*.
1:20 Pss 69:25; 109:8.

chosen [25]as an apostle to replace Judas the traitor in this ministry, for he has deserted us and gone where he belongs.'[26]Then they cast lots, and in this way Matthias was chosen and became an apostle with the other eleven.

The Holy Spirit Comes

2On the day of Pentecost, seven weeks after Jesus' resurrection,★ the believers were meeting together in one place. [2]Suddenly, there was a sound from heaven like the roaring of a mighty windstorm in the skies above them, and it filled the house where they were meeting. [3]Then, what looked like flames or tongues of fire appeared and settled on each of them. [4]And everyone present was filled with the Holy Spirit and began speaking in other languages,★ as the Holy Spirit gave them this ability.

[5]Godly Jews from many nations were living in Jerusalem at that time. [6]When they heard this sound, they came running to see what it was all about, and they were bewildered to hear their own languages being spoken by the believers.

[7]They were beside themselves with wonder. 'How can this be?' they exclaimed. 'These people are all from Galilee, [8]and yet we hear them speaking the languages of the lands where we were born! [9]Here we are – Parthians, Medes, Elamites, people from Mesopotamia, Judea, Capadocia,

---

[2:1] Greek *When the day of Pentecost arrived*. This annual celebration came 50 days after the Passover ceremonies. See Lev 23:16.
[2:4] Or *in other tongues*.

Pontus, the province of Asia, [10]Phrygia, Pamphylia, Egypt, and the areas of Libya toward Cyrene, visitors from Rome (both Jews and converts to Judaism), [11]Cretans, and Arabians. And we all hear these people speaking in our own languages about the wonderful things God has done!' [12]They stood there amazed and perplexed. 'What can this mean?' they asked each other. [13]But others in the crowd were mocking. 'They're drunk, that's all!' they said.

Peter Preaches to a Crowd

[14]Then Peter stepped forward with the eleven other apostles and shouted to the crowd, 'Listen carefully, all of you, fellow Jews and residents of Jerusalem! Make no mistake about this. [15]Some of you are saying these people are drunk. It isn't true! It's much too early for that. People don't get drunk by nine o'clock in the morning. [16]No, what you see this morning was predicted centuries ago by the prophet Joel:

[17]"In the last days, God said,
   I will pour out my Spirit upon all people.
  Your sons and daughters will prophesy,
     your young men will see visions,
     and your old men will dream dreams.
[18]In those days I will pour out my Spirit
     upon all my servants, men and women alike,
     and they will prophesy.
[19]And I will cause wonders in the heavens above
     and signs on the earth below –
     blood and fire and clouds of smoke.

²⁰The sun will be turned into darkness,

and the moon will turn bloodred,

before that great and glorious day of the Lord arrives.
²¹And anyone who calls on the name of the Lord will be
saved."⋆

²²'People of Israel, listen! God publicly endorsed Jesus of
Nazareth by doing wonderful miracles, wonders, and signs
through him, as you well know. ²³But you followed God's
prearranged plan. With the help of lawless Gentiles, you
nailed him to the cross and murdered him. ²⁴However, God
released him from the horrors of death and raised him back
to life again, for death could not keep him in its grip. ²⁵King
David said this about him:

"I know the Lord is always with me.

I will not be shaken, for he is right beside me.
²⁶No wonder my heart is filled with joy,

and my mouth shouts his praises!

My body rests in hope.
²⁷For you will not leave my soul among the dead⋆

or allow your Holy One to rot in the grave.
²⁸You have shown me the way of life,

and you will give me wonderful joy in your

presence."⋆

²⁹'Dear brothers, think about this! David wasn't referring to himself when he spoke these words I have quoted,
for he died and was buried, and his tomb is still here among
us. ³⁰But he was a prophet, and he knew God had promised

2:17-21 Joel 2:28–32.

2:27 Greek *in Hades*; also in 2:31.

2:25-28 Ps 16:8–11.

with an oath that one of David's own descendants would sit on David's throne as the Messiah. [31]David was looking into the future and predicting the Messiah's resurrection. He was saying that the Messiah would not be left among the dead and that his body would not rot in the grave.

[32]'This prophecy was speaking of Jesus, whom God raised from the dead, and we all are witnesses of this. [33]Now he sits on the throne of highest honor in heaven, at God's right hand. And the Father, as he had promised, gave him the Holy Spirit to pour out upon us, just as you see and hear today. [34]For David himself never ascended into heaven, yet he said,

> "The LORD said to my Lord,
> Sit in honor at my right hand
> [35] until I humble your enemies,
>   making them a footstool under your feet."★

[36]So let it be clearly known by everyone in Israel that God has made this Jesus whom you crucified to be both Lord and Messiah!'

[37]Peter's words convicted them deeply, and they said to him and to the other apostles, 'Brothers, what should we do?'

[38]Peter replied, 'Each of you must turn from your sins and turn to God, and be baptized in the name of Jesus Christ for the forgiveness of your sins. Then you will receive the gift of the Holy Spirit. [39]This promise is to you and to your children, and even to the Gentiles★ – all who have been called by the Lord our God.' [40]Then Peter

---

2:34-35 Ps 110:1.
2:39 Greek *to those far away.*

continued preaching for a long time, strongly urging all his listeners, 'Save yourselves from this generation that has gone astray!'

[41] Those who believed what Peter said were baptized and added to the church – about three thousand in all. [42] They joined with the other believers and devoted themselves to the apostles' teaching and fellowship, sharing in the Lord's Supper and in prayer.

The Believers Meet Together

[43] A deep sense of awe came over them all, and the apostles performed many miraculous signs and wonders. [44] And all the believers met together constantly and shared everything they had. [45] They sold their possessions and shared the proceeds with those in need. [46] They worshiped together at the Temple each day, met in homes for the Lord's Supper, and shared their meals with great joy and generosity – [47] all the while praising God and enjoying the goodwill of all the people. And each day the Lord added to their group those who were being saved.

Peter Heals a Crippled Beggar

3 Peter and John went to the Temple one afternoon to take part in the three o'clock prayer service. [2] As they approached the Temple, a man lame from birth was being carried in. Each day he was put beside the Temple gate, the one called the Beautiful Gate, so he could beg from the people going into the Temple. [3] When he saw Peter and John about to enter, he asked them for some money.

[4]Peter and John looked at him intently, and Peter said, 'Look at us!' [5]The lame man looked at them eagerly, expecting a gift. [6]But Peter said, 'I don't have any money for you. But I'll give you what I have. In the name of Jesus Christ of Nazareth, get up and walk!'

[7]Then Peter took the lame man by the right hand and helped him up. And as he did, the man's feet and ankle-bones were healed and strengthened. [8]He jumped up, stood on his feet, and began to walk! Then, walking, leaping, and praising God, he went into the Temple with them.

[9]All the people saw him walking and heard him praising God. [10]When they realized he was the lame beggar they had seen so often at the Beautiful Gate, they were absolutely astounded! [11]They all rushed out to Solomon's Colonnade, where he was holding tightly to Peter and John. Everyone stood there in awe of the wonderful thing that had happened.

Peter Preaches in the Temple

[12]Peter saw his opportunity and addressed the crowd. 'People of Israel,' he said, 'what is so astounding about this? And why look at us as though we had made this man walk by our own power and godliness? [13]For it is the God of Abraham, the God of Isaac, the God of Jacob, the God of all our ancestors who has brought glory to his servant Jesus by doing this. This is the same Jesus whom you handed over and rejected before Pilate, despite Pilate's decision to release him. [14]You rejected this holy, righteous one and instead demanded the release of a murderer. [15]You killed the author of life, but God raised him to life. And we are witnesses of this fact!

[16]'The name of Jesus has healed this man – and you know how lame he was before. Faith in Jesus' name has caused this healing before your very eyes.

[17]'Friends,* I realize that what you did to Jesus was done in ignorance; and the same can be said of your leaders. [18]But God was fulfilling what all the prophets had declared about the Messiah beforehand – that he must suffer all these things. [19]Now turn from your sins and turn to God, so you can be cleansed of your sins. [20]Then wonderful times of refreshment will come from the presence of the Lord, and he will send Jesus your Messiah to you again.

[21]For he must remain in heaven until the time for the final restoration of all things, as God promised long ago through his prophets. [22]Moses said, 'The Lord your God will raise up a Prophet like me from among your own people. Listen carefully to everything he tells you.'* [23]Then Moses said, 'Anyone who will not listen to that Prophet will be cut off from God's people and utterly destroyed.'*

[24]'Starting with Samuel, every prophet spoke about what is happening today.

[25]You are the children of those prophets, and you are included in the covenant God promised to your ancestors. For God said to Abraham, "Through your descendants all the families on earth will be blessed".*

[26]When God raised up his servant, he sent him first to you people of Israel, to bless you by turning each of you back from your sinful ways.'

[3:17] Greek *Brothers*.

[3:22] Deut 18:15.

[3:23] Deut 18:19; Lev 23:29.

[3:25] Gen 22:18.

Peter and John before the Council

4 While Peter and John were speaking to the people, the leading priests, the captain of the Temple guard, and some of the Sadducees came over to them. ²They were very disturbed that Peter and John were claiming, on the authority of Jesus, that there is a resurrection of the dead. ³They arrested them and, since it was already evening, jailed them until morning. ⁴But many of the people who heard their message believed it, so that the number of believers totaled about five thousand men, not counting women and children.★

⁵The next day the council of all the rulers and elders and teachers of religious law met in Jerusalem. ⁶Annas the high priest was there, along with Caiaphas, John, Alexander, and other relatives of the high priest. ⁷They brought in the two disciples and demanded, 'By what power, or in whose name, have you done this?'

⁸Then Peter, filled with the Holy Spirit, said to them, 'Leaders and elders of our nation, ⁹are we being questioned because we've done a good deed for a crippled man? Do you want to know how he was healed? ¹⁰Let me clearly state to you and to all the people of Israel that he was healed in the name and power of Jesus Christ from Nazareth, the man you crucified, but whom God raised from the dead. ¹¹For Jesus is the one referred to in the Scriptures, where it says,

> "The stone that you builders rejected has now become the cornerstone."★

---

^{4:4} Greek *5,000 adult males.*
^{4:11} Ps 118:22.

[12]There is salvation in no one else! There is no other name in all of heaven for people to call on to save them.'

[13]The members of the council were amazed when they saw the boldness of Peter and John, for they could see that they were ordinary men who had had no special training. They also recognized them as men who had been with Jesus. [14]But since the man who had been healed was standing right there among them, the council had nothing to say.

[15]So they sent Peter and John out of the council chamber★ and conferred among themselves.

[16]'What should we do with these men?' they asked each other. 'We can't deny they have done a miraculous sign, and everybody in Jerusalem knows about it. [17]But perhaps we can stop them from spreading their propaganda. We'll warn them not to speak to anyone in Jesus' name again.' [18]So they called the apostles back in and told them never again to speak or teach about Jesus.

[19]But Peter and John replied, 'Do you think God wants us to obey you rather than him? [20]We cannot stop telling about the wonderful things we have seen and heard.'

[21]The council then threatened them further, but they finally let them go because they didn't know how to punish them without starting a riot. For everyone was praising God [22]for this miraculous sign – the healing of a man who had been lame for more than forty years.

4:15 Greek *the Sanhedrin*.

The Believers Pray for Courage

[23] As soon as they were freed, Peter and John found the other believers and told them what the leading priests and elders had said. [24] Then all the believers were united as they lifted their voices in prayer: 'O Sovereign Lord, Creator of heaven and earth, the sea, and everything in them – [25] you spoke long ago by the Holy Spirit through our ancestor King David, your servant, saying,

"Why did the nations rage?
    Why did the people waste their time with futile plans?
[26] The kings of the earth prepared for battle;
    the rulers gathered together against
the Lord
    and against his Messiah."★

[27] 'That is what has happened here in this city! For Herod Antipas, Pontius Pilate the governor, the Gentiles, and the people of Israel were all united against Jesus, your holy servant, whom you anointed. [28] In fact, everything they did occurred according to your eternal will and plan. [29] And now, O Lord, hear their threats, and give your servants great boldness in their preaching. [30] Send your healing power; may miraculous signs and wonders be done through the name of your holy servant Jesus.'

[31] After this prayer, the building where they were meeting shook, and they were all filled with the Holy Spirit. And they preached God's message with boldness.

4:25–26 Ps 2:1–2.

The Believers Share Their Possessions

³²All the believers were of one heart and mind, and they felt that what they owned was not their own; they shared everything they had. ³³And the apóstles gave powerful witness to the resurrection of the Lord Jesus, and God's great favor was upon them all. ³⁴There was no poverty among them, because people who owned land or houses sold them ³⁵and brought the money to the apostles to give to others in need.

³⁶For instance, there was Joseph, the one the apostles nicknamed Barnabas (which means 'Son of Encouragement'). He was from the tribe of Levi and came from the island of Cyprus. ³⁷He sold a field he owned and brought the money to the apostles for those in need.

Ananias and Sapphira

5 There was also a man named Ananias who, with his wife, Sapphira, sold some property. ²He brought part of the money to the apostles, but he claimed it was the full amount. His wife had agreed to this deception.

³Then Peter said, 'Ananias, why has Satan filled your heart? You lied to the Holy Spirit, and you kept some of the money for yourself. ⁴The property was yours to sell or not sell, as you wished. And after selling it, the money was yours to give away. How could you do a thing like this? You weren't lying to us but to God.'

⁵As soon as Ananias heard these words, he fell to the floor and died. Everyone who heard about it was terrified. ⁶Then some young men wrapped him in a sheet and took him out and buried him.

[7]About three hours later his wife came in, not knowing what had happened. [8]Peter asked her, 'Was this the price you and your husband received for your land?'

'Yes,' she replied, 'that was the price.'

[9]And Peter said, 'How could the two of you even think of doing a thing like this – conspiring together to test the Spirit of the Lord? Just outside that door are the young men who buried your husband, and they will carry you out, too.'

[10]Instantly, she fell to the floor and died. When the young men came in and saw that she was dead, they carried her out and buried her beside her husband. [11]Great fear gripped the entire church and all others who heard what had happened.

The Apostles Heal Many

[12]Meanwhile, the apostles were performing many miraculous signs and wonders among the people. And the believers were meeting regularly at the Temple in the area known as Solomon's Colonnade. [13]No one else dared to join them, though everyone had high regard for them. [14]And more and more people believed and were brought to the Lord – crowds of both men and women. [15]As a result of the apostles' work, sick people were brought out into the streets on beds and mats so that Peter's shadow might fall across some of them as he went by. [16]Crowds came in from the villages around Jerusalem, bringing their sick and those possessed by evil spirits, and they were all healed.

The Apostles Meet Opposition

[17]The high priest and his friends, who were Sadducees, reacted with violent jealousy. [18]They arrested the apostles

and put them in the jail. ¹⁹But an angel of the Lord came at night, opened the gates of the jail, and brought them out. Then he told them, ²⁰'Go to the Temple and give the people this message of life!' ²¹So the apostles entered the Temple about daybreak and immediately began teaching.

When the high priest and his officials arrived, they convened the high council,⋆ along with all the elders of Israel. Then they sent for the apostles to be brought for trial. ²²But when the Temple guards went to the jail, the men were gone. So they returned to the council and reported, ²³'The jail was locked, with the guards standing outside, but when we opened the gates, no one was there!'

²⁴When the captain of the Temple guard and the leading priests heard this, they were perplexed, wondering where it would all end. ²⁵Then someone arrived with the news that the men they had jailed were out in the Temple, teaching the people.

²⁶The captain went with his Temple guards and arrested them, but without violence, for they were afraid the people would kill them if they treated the apostles roughly. ²⁷Then they brought the apostles in before the council. ²⁸'Didn't we tell you never again to teach in this man's name?' the high priest demanded. 'Instead, you have filled all Jerusalem with your teaching about Jesus, and you intend to blame us for his death!'

²⁹But Peter and the apostles replied, 'We must obey God rather than human authority. ³⁰The God of our ancestors raised Jesus from the dead after you killed him by crucifying him. ³¹Then God put him in the place of honor at his right hand as Prince and Savior. He did this to give the people of Israel an opportunity to turn from their sins and

---

⁵:²¹ Greek *Sanhedrin*; also in 5:27, 41.

turn to God so their sins would be forgiven. [32]We are witnesses of these things and so is the Holy Spirit, who is given by God to those who obey him.'

[33]At this, the high council was furious and decided to kill them. [34]But one member had a different perspective. He was a Pharisee named Gamaliel, who was an expert on religious law and was very popular with the people. He stood up and ordered that the apostles be sent outside the council chamber for a while. [35]Then he addressed his colleagues as follows: 'Men of Israel, take care what you are planning to do to these men! [36]Some time ago there was that fellow Theudas, who pretended to be someone great. About four hundred others joined him, but he was killed, and his followers went their various ways. The whole movement came to nothing. [37]After him, at the time of the census, there was Judas of Galilee. He got some people to follow him, but he was killed, too, and all his followers were scattered.

[38]'So my advice is, leave these men alone. If they are teaching and doing these things merely on their own, it will soon be overthrown. [39]But if it is of God, you will not be able to stop them. You may even find yourselves fighting against God.'

[40]The council accepted his advice. They called in the apostles and had them flogged. Then they ordered them never again to speak in the name of Jesus, and they let them go. [41]The apostles left the high council rejoicing that God had counted them worthy to suffer dishonor for the name of Jesus. [42]And every day, in the Temple and in their homes,★ they continued to teach and preach this message: 'The Messiah you are looking for is Jesus.'

5:42 Greek *from house to house.*

The Bible Jesus Read

Philip Yancey

Philip Yancey has a way of confronting our most cherished but misguided notions about faith. His award-winning books have inspired many to go deeper into God's Word.

In *The Bible Jesus Read*, he challenges the perception that the New Testament is all that matters and the Old Testament isn't worth taking time to read and understand.

As you explore the Old Testament books – Job, Deuteronomy, Psalms, Ecclesiastes, and the Prophets, you gain a new understanding of Christ, for these are the prayers, poems, songs, and bedtime stories that Jesus so revered.

'The more we comprehend the Old Testament,' Philip writes, 'the more we comprehend Jesus.'

And after all, shouldn't this be our goal?

Zondervan
ISBN: 0-3102-3186-8

Price: £8.99

Is the Old Testament Worth the Effort?

Faith is not the clinging to a shrine but an endless pilgrimage of the heart. Audacious longing, burning songs, daring thoughts, an impulse overwhelming the heart, usurping the mind – these are all a drive toward [loving the One] who rings our heart like a bell.
Abraham Heschel

My brother, who attended a Bible College during a smart-alecky phase in his life, enjoyed shocking groups of believers by sharing his 'life verse.' After listening to others quote pious phrases from Proverbs, Romans, or Ephesians, he would stand and with a perfectly straight face recite this verse very rapidly:

At Parbar westward, four at the causeway, and two at Par-bar. 1 Chronicles 26:18.

Other students would screw up their faces and wonder what deep spiritual insight they were missing. Perhaps he was speaking another language?

If my brother felt in a particularly ornery mood, he would quote an alternative verse:

O daughter of Babylon . . . Happy shall he be, that taketh and
dasheth thy little ones against the stones. Psalm 137:9.

In his sassiness my brother had, quite ingeniously, iden-
tified the two main barriers to reading the Old Testament:
It doesn't always make sense, and what sense it does make
offends modern ears. For these and other reasons the Old
Testament, three-fourths of the Bible, often goes unread.

As a result, knowledge of the Old Testament is fading
fast among Christians and has virtually vanished in popular
culture. In a comedy routine Jay Leno tested his audience's
knowledge of the Bible by asking them to name one of the
Ten Commandments. A hand shot up: 'God helps those
who help themselves?' Everybody laughed, but no one else
could do better. Polls show that eighty percent of Americans claim to believe in the Ten Commandments, but very
few can name as many as four of them. Half of all adult
Americans cannot identify the Bible's first book as Genesis.
And fourteen percent identify Joan of Arc as Noah's wife.

More surprisingly, a Wheaton College professor named
Gary Burge has found that ignorance of the Old Testament
extends to the church as well. For several years Burge has
been testing incoming freshman at his school, a premier
evangelical institution. His surveys show that students who
have attended Sunday School all their lives, have watched
innumerable episodes of *Veggie Tales*, and have listened to
countless sermons, cannot identify basic facts about the
Old Testament.

The experience of Barry Taylor, former rock musician
and now pastor, suggests a reason. He told me, 'In the early
1970s my best friend became a Jesus freak. I thought he was
crazy, so I started searching the Bible in order to find argu-
ments to refute him. For the life of me, I could not figure

out why God was concerned with the bent wing of a dove, or why he would give an order to kill, say, 40,000 Amalekites. And who were the Amalekites anyway? Fortunately I kept reading, plowing through all the hard books. When I got to the New Testament, I couldn't find a way around Jesus. So I became a Jesus freak too.'

I am glad Barry Taylor made it to Jesus, but I recognize that he raises some good questions in the process. Why does the Bible spend so much time on temples, priests, and rules governing sacrifices that no longer even exist? Why does God care about defective sacrificial animals – limping lambs and bent-winged doves – or about a young goat cooked in its mother's milk, and yet apparently not about people like the Amalekites? How can we make sense of the strange Old Testament, and how does it apply to our lives today? In short, is the Old Testament worth the effort it takes to read and understand it?

I have heard from missionaries in places like Africa and Afghanistan that people there respond immediately to the Old Testament, for its stories of land disputes, water rights, tribal feuds, and arranged marriages relate directly to how they live now. But such customs are far removed from a Greek-thinking sophisticate like the apostle Paul, and much further removed from the average suburbanite living, say, in Tampa, Florida. Those of us in developed countries who pick up the Old Testament and simply start reading may well feel boredom, confusion, or even outrage at the violence portrayed there. Jesus we identify with, the apostle Paul we think we understand, but what of those barbaric people living in the Middle East several thousand years ago? What to make of them?

Most people get around this dilemma by avoiding the Old Testament entirely. Or, perhaps worse, they mine it for a nugget of truth that can be extracted and held up to the light, like a diamond plucked from a vein of coal. That technique can backfire, however – remember my brother's life verses.

I can think of one ironic 'advantage' to ignorance of the Old Testament. 'The man of today ... must read the Scriptures as though they were something entirely unfamiliar, as though they had not been set before him ready-made,' wrote the Jewish scholar Martin Buber. Buber is now getting his wish: most people of today *do* read the Old Testament as something entirely unfamiliar!

Why Bother?

This book recounts how I came to stop avoiding and start reading – ultimately loving – the Old Testament. I confess that I began with ignoble motives: I read it because I was paid to, as part of my editorial assignment to produce *The Student Bible*. Long after *The Student Bible* had been published and stocked on bookstore shelves, however, I kept returning to the Old Testament on my own.

My reading experience parallels one I had with William Shakespeare. In a moment of idealism, I made a New Year's resolution to read all thirty-eight of Shakespeare's plays in one year. Due to travel, a cross-country move, and other interruptions, I had to extend that deadline. Yet, to my surprise, fulfilling the task seemed far more like entertainment than like work. At first I had to look up archaic words, concentrate on keeping the characters straight, and adjust to the sheer awkwardness of reading plays. I found, though, that as I kept at it and got accustomed to the rhythm and language, these distractions faded and I felt myself being swept up in the play. Without fail I looked forward to the designated Shakespeare evenings.

I expected to learn about Shakespeare's world and the people who inhabited it. I found, though, that Shakespeare mainly taught me about *my* world. He endures as a playwright because of his genius in probing the hidden recesses of humanity, a skill that gives him appeal in places as varied as the United States, China, and Peru several centuries after his death. We find ourselves in his plays.

I went through precisely that same process in encountering the Old Testament. From initial resistance, I moved to a reluctant sense that I *ought* to read the neglected three-quarters of the Bible. As I worked past some of the barriers (much like learning to read Shakespeare), I came to feel a *need* to read, because of what it was teaching me. Eventually I found myself *wanting* to read those thirty-nine books, which were satisfying in me some hunger that nothing else had – not even, I must say, the New Testament. They taught me about Life with God: not how it is supposed to work, but how it actually does work.

The rewards offered by the Old Testament do not come easily, I admit. Learning to feel at home in its pages will take time and effort. All achievements – climbing mountains, mastering the guitar, competing in a triathlon – require a similar process of hard work; we persevere because we believe rewards will come.

A reader of the Old Testament confronts obstacles not present in other books. For example, I was put off at first by its disarray. The Old Testament does not read like a cohesive novel; it consists of poetry, history, sermons, and short stories written by various authors and mixed up together. In its time, of course, no one conceived of the Old Testament as one book. Each book had its own scroll, and a long book like

Jeremiah would occupy a scroll twenty or thirty feet long. A
Jewish person entering a synagogue would see stacks of
scrolls, not a single book, and, aware of their differences,
would choose accordingly. (Indeed, on certain solemn holi-
days Jews were only permitted to read from Job, Jeremiah,
and Lamentations in order to stay appropriately mournful;
the other books might provide too much pleasure.)

Yet I find it remarkable that this diverse collection of
manuscripts written over a period of a millennium by several dozen authors possesses as much unity as it does. To
appreciate this feat, imagine a book begun five hundred
years before Columbus and just now completed. The
Bible's striking unity is one strong sign that God directed
its composition. By using a variety of authors and cultural
situations, God developed a complete record of what he
wants us to know; amazingly, the parts fit together in such a
way that a single story does emerge.

The more I persevered, the more passages I came to
understand. And the more I understood, the more I found
myself in those passages. Even in a culture as secular as the
United States, best-sellers such as *Care of the Soul* by Thomas
Moore and *The Cloister Walk* by Kathleen Norris reveal a
deep spiritual hunger. The Old Testament speaks to that
hunger like no other book. It does not give us a lesson in theology, with abstract concepts neatly arranged in logical order.
Quite the opposite: it gives an advanced course in Life with
God, expressed in a style at once personal and passionate.

Neither Testament Is Enough

Christians of all stripes hold one thing in common: we believe the Old Testament is not enough. Jesus the Messiah

came to introduce a 'New Covenant,' or New Testament, and following the apostle Paul we look back on the Old Testament period as a time of preparation. Without question I agree. Yet I am increasingly convinced that neither is the New Testament enough. On its own, it proves insufficient for understanding God or our world.

When Thomas Cahill wrote the book *The Gifts of the Jews* he chose the subtitle, 'How a Tribe of Desert Nomads Changed the Way Everyone Thinks and Feels.' He is surely right. Western civilization builds so directly on foundations laid in the Old Testament era that it would not otherwise make sense. As Cahill points out, the Jewish belief in monotheism gave us a Great Whole, a unified universe that can, as a product of one Creator, be studied and manipulated scientifically. Ironically, our technological modern world traces back to that tribe of desert nomads.

The Jews also gave us what Cahill calls the Conscience of the West, the belief that God expresses himself not primarily through outward show, but rather through the 'still, small voice' of conscience. A God of love and compassion, he cares about all of his creatures, especially human beings created 'in his own image,' and he asks us to do the same. Every person on earth has inherent human dignity. Following that God, the Jews gave us a pattern for the great liberation movements of modern history, and for just laws to protect the weak and minorities and the oppressed.

According to Cahill, without the Jews,

. . . we would never have known the abolitionist movement, the prison-reform movement, the antiwar movement, the labor movement, the civil rights movement, the movements of indigenous and dispossessed peoples for their human rights, the antiapartheid movement in South Africa, the Solidarity movement in Poland, the free-speech and pro-democracy movements in such Far Eastern countries as South Korea, the Philippines, and even China.

So many of the concepts and words we use daily – new, individual, person, history, freedom, spirit, justice, time, faith, pilgrimage, revolution – derive from the Old Testament that we can hardly imagine the world and our place in it without relying on the Jewish heritage. A comic character in one of Molière's plays suddenly discovers, 'I am speaking prose! I am speaking prose!' Our roots go so deep in Old Testament thinking that in many ways – human rights, government, the treatment of neighbors, our understanding of God – we are already speaking and thinking Old Testament.

Most assuredly we cannot understand the New Testament apart from the Old. The proof is simple: try understanding Hebrews, Jude, or Revelation without any reference to Old Testament allusions or concepts. It cannot be done (which may explain why many modern Christians avoid those books too). The Gospels can be read as stand-alone stories, but a reader unacquainted with the Old Testament will miss many layers of richness in them. Paul constantly appealed to the Old Testament. Without exception, every New Testament author wrote about the new work of God on earth while looking through the prism of the earlier or 'old' work.

A Chinese philosopher insisted on riding his mule backwards so that he would not be distracted by where he was going and could instead reflect on where he had been. The Bible works in somewhat the same way. The Epistles shed light backward on the events of the Gospels, so that we understand them in a new way. Epistles and Gospels both shed light backward on the Old Testament.

For centuries the phrase 'as predicted by the prophets' was one of the most powerful influences on people coming to faith. Justin the Martyr credited his conversion to the impression made on him by the Old Testament's predictive accuracy. The brilliant French mathematician Blaise Pascal also cited fulfilled prophecies as one of the most important factors in his faith. Nowadays, few Christians read the prophets except in search of Ouija-board-like clues into the future. We have lost the Reformers' profound sense of unity between the two testaments.

Understanding our civilization and understanding the Bible may be important reasons for reading the Old Testament, but the title of this book hints at perhaps the most important reason: It is the Bible Jesus read. He traced in its passages every important fact about himself and his mission. He quoted from it to settle controversies with opponents such as the Pharisees, Sadducees, and Satan himself. The images – Lamb of God, shepherd, sign of Jonah, stone which the builders rejected – that Jesus used to define himself came straight from the pages of the Old Testament.

Once, a government tried to amputate the Old Testament from Christian Scriptures. The Nazis in Germany forbade study of this 'Jewish book,' and Old Testament scholarship disappeared from German seminaries and journals. In 1940, at the height of Nazi power, Dietrich Bonhoeffer defiantly published a book on Psalms and got slapped with a fine. In letters of appeal he argued convincingly that he was explicating the prayer book of Jesus Christ himself. Jesus quoted often from the Old Testament, Bonhoeffer noted, and never from any other book – even though the Hebrew canon had not been officially closed. Besides, much of the Old Testament explicitly or implicitly points to Jesus.

When we read the Old Testament, we read the Bible Jesus read and used. These are the prayers Jesus prayed, the poems he memorized, the songs he sand, the bedtime stories he heard as a child, the prophecies he pondered. He revered every 'jot and tittle' of the Hebrew Scriptures. The more we comprehend the Old Testament, the more we comprehend Jesus. Said Martin Luther, 'the Old Testament is a testamental letter of Christ, which he caused to be opened after his death and read and proclaimed everywhere through the Gospel.'

In a poignant passage from his Gospel, Luke tells of Jesus spontaneously appearing by the side of two disciples on the road to Emmaus. Even though rumors of the Resurrection were spreading like wildfire, clearly these two did not yet believe, as Jesus could tell by looking into their downcast eyes. In a kind of practical joke, Jesus got them to repeat all that had happened to this man Jesus – they had not yet recognized him – over the past few days. Then he gave them a rebuke:

> 'How foolish you are, and how slow of heart to believe all that the prophets have spoken! Did not the Christ have to suffer these things and then enter his glory?' And beginning with Moses and all the Prophets, he explained to them what was said in all the Scriptures concerning himself.

Today we need an 'Emmaus road' experience in reverse. The disciples knew Moses and the Prophets but could not conceive how they might relate to Jesus the Christ. The modern church knows Jesus the Christ but is fast losing any grasp of Moses and the Prophets.

Elsewhere, Jesus told a story of two men who built houses that, from the outside, looked alike. The true difference between them came to light when a storm hit. One house did not fall, even though rain poured down, streams rose, and winds beat against it, because its foundation rested on rock. The second house, foolishly built on sand, fell with a great crash. In theology as well as in construction, foundations matter.

Quick, What Is God Like?

According to Elaine Storkey, that question, 'Quick, what is God like?' was asked by a five-year-old girl who rushed up to her newborn brother in his hospital room. She shrewdly figured that, having just come from Heaven, he might have some inside information. Alas, he merely made a gurgling sound and rolled his eyes.

The Old Testament provides an answer to the little girl's question, a different answer than we might get from the New Testament alone. Although Jesus is the 'image of the invisible God,' he emptied himself of many of the prerogatives of God in order to become a man. The late professor Langdon Gilkey used to say that if evangelical Christianity has a heresy it is the neglect of God the Father, the Creator, Preserver, and Ruler of all human history and every human community, in favor of Jesus the Son, who relates to individual souls and their destinies.

If we had only the Gospels, we would envision a God who seems confined, all-too-human, and rather weak – after all, Jesus ended up hanging on a cross. The Jews objected so strongly to Jesus because, despite his audacious claims, he did not match their conception of what God is like; they rejected him for not measuring up. The book of Revelation gives a different glimpse of Jesus – blazing light, stunning in glory, unlimited in power – and the Old Testament likewise fills in a different portrayal of God. Like Jesus' original disciples, we need that background picture in order to appreciate how much *love* the Incarnation expressed – how much God gave up on our behalf.

Apart from the Old Testament we will always have an impoverished view of God. God is not a philosophical construct but a Person who acts in history: the one who created Adam, who gave a promise to Noah, who called Abraham and introduced himself by name to Moses, who deigned to live in a wilderness *tent* in order to live close to his people. From Genesis 1 onward, God has wanted himself to be known, and the Old Testament is our most complete revelation of what God is like.

John Updike has said that 'our brains are no longer conditioned for reverence and awe.' The very words sound old-fashioned, and to the degree that they do, to that degree we have strayed from the picture of God revealed in the Old Testament. We cannot box him in, explain him away. God seems a wild and mysterious Other, not a God we can easily figure out. No one tells him what to do (the main point in God's blistering speech to Job).

I admit that the Old Testament introduces some problems I would rather avoid. Throughout this book I will struggle with the revelation of God I find there. 'Consider therefore the kindness and sternness of God,' wrote Paul to the Christians in Rome. I would rather consider only the kindness of God, but by doing so I would construct my own image of God instead of relying on God's self-revelation. I dare not speak for God without listening to God speak for himself.

It makes an enormous difference how we picture God. Is God an aloof watchmaker who winds up the universe and steps back to watch it wind down on its own? Or is God a caring parent who holds not just the universe but individual men and women in his hands? I cannot conceive of a more important project than restoring a proper notion of what God is like.

Unavoidably, we transfer to God feelings and reactions that come from our human parents. George Bernard Shaw had difficulty with God because his father had been a scoundrel, an absentee father who cared mostly about cricket and pubs. Likewise, C. S. Lewis struggled to overcome the imprint left by his own father, a harsh man who would resort to quoting Cicero to his children when scolding them. When his mother died, Lewis said, it felt as if Atlantis had broken off and left him stranded on a tiny island. After studying at a public school led by a cruel headmaster who was later certified insane and committed to an institution, Lewis had to overcome the impact of these male figures to find a way to love God.

The Old Testament portrays God as a father, yes, but a different kind of father than that encountered by Shaw and Lewis. It portrays God as a lion but also a lamb, an eagle but also a mother hen, a king but also a servant, a judge but also a shepherd. Just when we think we have God pinned down, the Old Testament introduces a whole new picture of him: as a whistler, a barber, a vineyard keeper.

Like a drumbeat that never stops, in the pages of the Old Testament we hear the consistent message that this world revolves around God, not us. The Hebrews had incessant reminders built into their culture. They dedicated their firstborn livestock and children to God, wore portions of the law on their heads and wrists, posted visible reminders on their doorways, said the word 'blessed' a hundred times a day, even wore distinctive hairstyles and sewed tassels on their garments. A devout Jew could barely make it through an hour, much less an entire day, without running smack into some reminder that he or she lived in God's world. Even the Hebrew calendar marked time by events such as the Passover and Day of Atonement, not merely by the harvest cycle and the moon. The world, they believed, is God's property. And human life is 'sacred,' which simply means that it belongs to God to do with what he wills.

This Old Testament notion sounds very un-American. Do not our founding documents guarantee us the right to life, liberty, and the pursuit of happiness? We rebel against any interference with our personal rights, and anyone who attempts to set boundaries that might encroach on our personal space. In our secularized, industrialized environment, we can go through an entire week, not just a day, without bumping into a reminder that this is God's world.

I remember hearing a chapel message at Wheaton College during the 1970s, when the Death of God movement had reached its peak. Professor Robert Webber chose to speak on the third commandment, 'Thou shalt not take the name of the Lord thy God in vain.' We usually interpret that commandment in a narrow sense of prohibiting swearing, said Webber, who then proceeded to expand its meaning to 'never live as though God does not exist.' Or, stated positively, 'Always live in awareness of God's existence.' The more I study the commandment in its Old Testament environment, the more I agree with Webber. Any key to living in such awareness must be found in the great Jewish legacy of the Old Testament.

I am not proposing that we return to forelocks, phylacteries, and a diet that excludes pork and lobster. Nevertheless, I do believe we have much to learn from a people whose daily lives centered on God. When we look back on the covenant between God and the ancient Hebrews, what stands out to us is its strictness, the seeming arbitrariness of some of its laws. I see no such reaction among the Hebrews themselves. Few of them pleaded with God to loosen the dietary restrictions or eliminate some of their religious obligations. They seemed, rather, *relieved* that their God, unlike the pagan gods around them, had agreed to define a relationship with them.

As the Puritan scholar Perry Miller has said, when you have a covenant with God, you no longer have an ineffable, remote, unapproachable Deity; you have a God you can count on. The Hebrews and God had entered into a kind of story together, and everything about their lives sent back echoes of that story. The story was a love story, from the very beginning. God chose them not because they were larger and stronger than other tribes – quite the contrary. Nor did he choose them for their moral superiority. He chose them because he loved them.

Like any starstruck lover, God yearned for a response. All the commands given the Hebrews flowed out of the very first commandment, 'Love the Lord your God with all your heart and with all your soul and with all your strength.' The Hebrews failed to keep that command, of course, but the reason Christians now call three-fourths of the Bible the 'Old' Testament is that not even that terrible failure could cancel out God's love. God found a new way – a new covenant, or testament, of his love.

Søren Kierkegaard offers two suggestions for the reader who tackles difficult portions of the Bible. First, read it like a love letter, he says. As you struggle with language, culture, and other barriers, look on them as the necessary work to get to the main, crucial message from someone who loves you. Second, act on what you do understand. Kierkegaard dismisses the objection 'There are so many obscure passages in the Holy Scriptures, whole books which are almost riddles' with the reply that he would only consider that objection from someone who had fully complied with all the passages that are easy to understand!

Is God Really Good?

For thousands of years the Jews have prayed this prayer: 'Give thanks to the Lord Almighty, for the Lord is good; his love endures forever.' It makes a good prayer to reflect on, because we doubt precisely those two things today. Is the Lord good? Does his love endure forever? A glance at history, or any day's headlines, and a reasonable person begins to wonder about those bold assertions. For this reason, too, the Old Testament merits our attention, because the Jews loudly doubted the very prayer they prayed. As befitting an intimate relationship, they took those doubts to the other party, to God himself, and got a direct response.

We learn from the Old Testament how God works, which is not at all as we might expect. God moves slowly, unpredictably, paradoxically. The first eleven chapters of Genesis describe a series of human failures that call the entire creation project into question. As a remedy to those failures, God declares a plan in Genesis 12: to deal with the general problem of humanity by establishing one particular family, a tribe known as the Hebrews (later called the Jews). Through them, the womb for the Incarnation, God will bring about restoration of the entire earth, back to its original design.

That plan declared, God proceeds in a most mysterious manner. To found his tribe, God chooses a pagan from the region that is now Iraq and puts him through a series of tests, many of which he fails. In Egypt, for example, Abraham demonstrates a morality inferior to that of the Sun worshipers.

After promising to bring about a people numerous as the stars in the sky and the sand on the seashore, God then proceeds to conduct a clinic in infertility. Abraham and Sarah wait into their nineties to see their first child; their daughter-in-law Rebekah proves barren for a time; her son Jacob must wait fourteen years for the wife of his dreams, only to discover her barren as well. Three straight generations of infertile women hardly seems an efficient way to populate a great nation.

After making similar promises to bring about possession of a great land (Abraham himself possessed only a grave site in Canaan), God arranges a detour for the Israelites into Egypt, where they molder for *four centuries* until Moses arrives to lead them to the Promised Land – a wretched journey that takes forty years instead of the expected two weeks. Clearly, God operates on a different timetable than that used by impatient human beings.

The surprises continue on into New Testament times, for none of the vaunted Jewish scholars recognizes Jesus of Nazareth as the Messiah trumpeted in the Psalms and Prophets. In fact, they continue today, as self-appointed prophets confidently identify a succession of tyrants and world figures as the Antichrist, only to see Hitler, Stalin, Kissinger, and Hussein fade from view.

Christians living today face many unfulfilled promises. World poverty and population continue to soar and, as a percentage of population, Christianity barely holds its own. The planet lurches toward self-destruction. We wait, and keep on waiting, for the glory days promised in the

Prophets and in Revelation. From Abraham and Joseph and Moses and David we gain at least the knowledge that God moves in ways we would not predict or even desire. At times God's history seems to operate on an entirely different plane than ours.

The Old Testament gives clues into the kind of history God is writing. Exodus identifies by name the two Hebrew midwives who helped save Moses' life, but it does not bother to record the name of the Pharaoh ruling Egypt (an omission that has baffled scholars ever since). First Kings grants a total of eight verses to King Omri, even though secular historians regard him as one of Israel's most powerful kings. In his own history, God does not seem impressed by size or power or wealth. Faith is what he wants, and the heroes who emerge are heroes of faith, not strength or wealth.

God's history thus focuses on those who hold faithful to him regardless of how things turn out. When Nebuchadnezzar, one of many tyrants who persecute the Jews, threatens three young men with torture by fire, they respond:

> If we are thrown into the blazing furnace, the God we serve is able to save us from it, and he will rescue us from your hand, O king. But even if he does not, we want you to know, O king, that we will not serve your gods or worship the image of gold you have set up.

Empires rise and fall, powerful leaders soar to power, then topple from it. The same Nebuchadnezzar who tossed these three into a fiery furnace ends up demented, grazing on grass in the field like a cow. The succession of empires that follow his — Persia, Greece, Rome — so mighty in their day, join the dustbin of history even as God's people the Jews survive murderous pogroms. Slowly, painstakingly, God writes his history on earth through the deeds of his faithful followers, one by one.

Out of their tortured history, the Jews demonstrate the most surprising lesson of all: you cannot go wrong personalizing God. God is not a blurry power living somewhere in the sky, not an abstraction like the Greeks proposed, not a sensual super-human like the Romans worshiped, and definitely not the absentee watchmaker of the Deists. God is *personal*. He enters into people's lives, messes with families, shows up in unexpected places, chooses unlikely leaders, calls people to account. Most of all, God loves.

As the great Jewish theologian Abraham Heschel put it in *The Prophets*,

> To the prophet, God does not reveal himself in an abstract absoluteness, but in a personal and intimate relation to the world. He does not simply command and expect obedience; He is also moved and affected by what happens in the world, and reacts accordingly. Events and human actions arouse in him joy or sorrow, pleasure or wrath. . . . Man's deeds may move Him, affect Him, grieve Him or, on the other hand, gladden and please Him.
>
> . . . the God of Israel is a God Who loves, a God Who is known to, and concerned with, man. He not only rules the world in the majesty of his might and wisdom, but reacts intimately to the events of history.

More than any other word pictures, God chooses 'children' and 'lovers' to describe our relationship with him as being intimate and personal. The Old Testament abounds with husband-bride imagery. God woos his people and dotes on them like a lover doting on his beloved. When they ignore him, he feels hurt, spurned, like a jilted lover. Shifting metaphors generationally, it also announces that we are God's children. In other words, the closest we can come to understanding how God looks upon us is by thinking about the people who mean most to us: our own child, our lover.

Think of a doting parent with a video camera, coaxing his year-old daughter to let go of the living room coffee table and take three steps toward him. 'Come on, sweetie, you can do it! Just let go. Daddy's here. Come on'. Think of a love-struck teenager with her phone permanently attached to her ear, reviewing every second of her day with a boy who is himself infatuated enough to be interested. Think of those two scenes and then imagine God on one end and you on the other. That is the message of the Old Testament.

The Power of a Praying Wife

Stormie Omartian

'I cannot imagine what my life would be without her praying for me,' says Michael Omartian. Stormie Omartian shares how God has strengthened their marriage since she began to pray for her husband.

'First of all,' she says, 'let me make it perfectly clear that the power of a praying wife is not a means of gaining control over your husband, so don't get your hopes up!'

Every aspect of her husband's life is covered by prayer from the most obvious – work, fatherhood, health and faith to the more hidden aspects of purpose, integrity, and temptations.

Along with real life examples, there are prayers and 'power tools' – inspiring verses to remind wives that God is working for renewal and growth in marriage.

Kingsway Publications
ISBN: 0-8547-6759-2

Price: £5.99

The Power

First of all, let me make it perfectly clear that the power of a praying wife is not a means of gaining control over your husband, so don't get your hopes up! In fact, it is quite the opposite. It's laying down all claim to power in and of yourself, and relying on God's power to transform you, your husband, your circumstances, and your marriage. This power is not given to wield like a weapon in order to beat back an unruly beast. It's a gentle tool of restoration appropriated through the prayers of a wife who longs to do right more than be right, and to *give life* more than *get even*. It's a way to invite God's power into your husband's life for his greatest blessing, which is ultimately yours, too.

When my husband, Michael, and I were first married and differences arose between us, praying was definitely not my first thought. In fact, it was closer to a last resort. I tried other methods first such as arguing, pleading, ignoring, avoiding, confronting, debating, and of course the ever-popular silent treatment, all with far less than satisfying results. It took some time to realize that by praying *first*, these unpleasant methods of operation could be avoided.

By the time you read this book, Michael and I will have been married over a quarter of a century. This is nothing less than miraculous. It's certainly not a testimony to our greatness, but to God's faithfulness to answer prayer. I confess that even after all these years, I am still learning about this and it doesn't come easy. While I may not have as much practice doing it right as I have had doing it wrong, I can say without reservation that *prayer works*.

Unfortunately, I didn't learn how to *really* pray for my husband until I started praying for my children. As I saw profound answers to prayer for them, I decided to try being just as detailed and fervent in praying for him. But I found that praying for children is far easier. From the first moment we lay eyes on them, we want the best for their lives – unconditionally, wholeheartedly, without question. But with a husband, it's often not that simple – especially for someone who's been married awhile. A husband can hurt your feelings, be inconsiderate, uncaring, abusive, irritating, or negligent. He can say or do things that pierce your heart like a sliver. And every time you start to pray for him, you find the sliver festering. It's obvious you can't give yourself to praying the way God wants you to until you are rid of it.

Praying for your husband is not the same as praying for a child (even though it may seem similar), because you are not your husband's mother. We have authority over our children that is given to us by the Lord. We *don't* have authority over our husbands. However, we have been given authority 'over all the power of the enemy' (Luke 10:19) and can do great damage to the enemy's plans when we pray. Many difficult things that happen in a marriage relationship are actually part of the enemy's plan set up for its demise. But we can say, 'I will not allow anything to destroy my marriage.'

'I will not stand by and watch my husband be wearied, beaten down, or destroyed.'

'I will not sit idle while an invisible wall goes up between us.'

'I will not allow confusion, miscommunication, wrong attitudes, and bad choices to erode what we are trying to build together.'

'I will not tolerate hurt and unforgiveness leading us to divorce.' We can take a stand against any negative influences in our marriage relationship and know that God has given us authority in His name to back it up.

You have the means to establish a hedge of protection around your marriage because Jesus said, 'Whatever you bind on earth will be bound in heaven, and whatever you loose on earth will be loosed in heaven' (Matthew 18:18). You have authority in the name of Jesus to *stop evil* and *permit good*. You can submit to God in prayer whatever controls your husband – alcoholism, workaholism, laziness, depression, infirmity, abusiveness, anxiety, fear, or failure – and pray for him to be released from it..

Wait! Before You Write Off the Marriage . . .

I confess right now that there was a time when I considered separation or divorce. This is an embarrassing disclosure because I don't believe either of those options is the best answer to a troubled marriage. I believe in God's position on divorce. He says it's not right and it grieves Him. The last thing I want to do is grieve God. But I know what it's like to feel the kind of despair that paralyzes good decision making. I've experienced the degree of hopelessness that causes a person to give up on trying to do what's right. I understand the torture of loneliness that leaves you longing for anyone who will look into your soul and see *you*.

I've felt pain so bad that the fear of dying from it propelled me to seek out the only immediately foreseeable means of survival: escape from the source of agony. I know what it's like to contemplate acts of desperation because you see no future. I've experienced such a buildup of negative emotions day after day that separation and divorce seemed like nothing more than the promise of pleasant relief.

The biggest problem I faced in our marriage was my husband's temper. The only ones who were ever the object of his anger were me and the children. He used words like weapons that left me crippled or paralyzed. I'm not saying that I was without fault – quite the contrary. I was sure I was as much to blame as he, but I didn't know what to do about it. I pleaded with God on a regular basis to make my husband more sensitive, less angry, more pleasant, less irritable. But I saw few changes. Was God not listening? Or did He favor the husband over the wife, as I suspected?

After a number of years, with little change, I cried out to the Lord one day in despair, saying, 'God, I can't live this way anymore. I know what You've said about divorce, but I can't live in the same house with him. Help me, Lord.' I sat on the bed holding my Bible for hours as I struggled with the strongest desire to take the children and leave. I believe that because I came to God in total honesty about what I felt, He allowed me to thoroughly and clearly envision what life would be like if I left: Where I would live, how I would support myself and care for the children, who would still be my friends, and worst of all, how a heritage of divorce would affect my son and daughter. It was the most horrible and unspeakably sad picture. If I left I would find some relief, but at the price of everything dear to me. I knew it wasn't God's plan for us.

As I sat there, God also impressed upon my heart that if I

would deliberately lay down my life before His throne, die to the desire to leave, and give my needs to Him, He would teach me how to lay down my life in prayer for Michael. He would show me how to really intercede for him as a son of God, and in the process He would revive my marriage and pour His blessings out on both of us. We would be better together, if could get past this, than we could ever be separated and alone. He showed me that Michael was caught in a web from his past that rendered him incapable of being different from what he was at that moment, but God would use me as an instrument of His deliverance if I would consent to it. It hurt to say yes to this and I cried a lot. But when I did, I felt hopeful for the first time in years.

I began to pray every day for Michael, like I had never prayed before. Each time, though, I had to confess my own hardness of heart. I saw how deeply hurt and unforgiving of him I was. *I don't want to pray for him. I don't want to ask God to bless him. I only want God to strike his heart with lightning and convict him of how cruel he has been*, I thought. I had to say over and over, 'God, I confess my unforgiveness toward my husband. Deliver me from all of it.'

Little by little, I began to see changes occur in both of us. When Michael became angry, instead of reacting negatively, I prayed for him. I asked God to give me insight into what was causing his rage. He did. I asked Him what I could do to make things better. He showed me. My husband's anger became less frequent and more quickly soothed. Every day, prayer built something positive. We're still not perfected, but we've come a long way. It hasn't been easy, yet I'm convinced that God's way is worth the effort it takes to walk in it. It's the only way to save a marriage.

A wife's prayers for her husband have a far greater effect on him than anyone else's, even his mother's. (Sorry,

Mom.) A mother's prayers for her child are certainly fervent. But when a man marries, he leaves his father and mother and becomes one with his wife (Matthew 19:5). They are a team, one unit, unified in spirit. The strength of a man and wife joined together in God's sight is *far* greater than the sum of the strengths of each of the two individuals. That's because the Holy Spirit unites them and gives added power to their prayers.

That's also why there is so much at stake if we *don't* pray. Can you imagine praying for the right side of your body and not the left? If the right side is not sustained and protected and it falls, it's going to bring down the left side with it. The same is true of you and your husband. If you pray for yourself and not him, you will never find the blessings and fulfillment you want. What happens to him happens to you and you can't get around it.

This oneness gives us a power that the enemy doesn't like. That's why he devises ways to weaken it. He gives us whatever we will fall for, whether it be low self-esteem, pride, the need to be right, miscommunication, or the bowing to our own selfish desires. He will tell you lies like, 'Nothing will ever change.' 'Your failures are irreparable.' 'There's no hope for reconciliation.' 'You'd be happier with someone else.' He'll tell you whatever you will believe, because he knows if he can get you to believe it, there is no future for your marriage. If you believe enough lies, your heart will eventually be hardened against God's truth.

In every broken marriage, there is at least one person whose heart is hard against God. When a heart becomes hard, there is no vision from God's perspective. When we're miserable in a marriage, we feel that anything will be an improvement over what we're experiencing. But we don't see the whole picture. We only see the way it is, not the way God wants it to become. When we pray, however, our hearts become *soft* toward God and we get a vision. We see there is hope. We have faith that He will restore all that has been devoured, destroyed, and eaten away from the marriage. 'I will restore to you the years that the swarming locust has eaten' (Joel 2:25). We can trust Him to take away the pain, hopelessness, hardness, and unforgiveness. We are able to envision His ability to resurrect love and life from the deadest of places.

Imagine Mary Magdalene's joy when she went to Jesus' tomb the morning after He had been crucified and found that He was not dead after all, but had been raised up by the power of God. The joy of seeing something hopelessly dead brought to life is the greatest joy we can know. The power that resurrected Jesus is the very same power that will resurrect the dead places of your marriage and put life back into it. 'God both raised up the Lord and will also raise us up by His power' (1 Corinthians 6:14). It's the only power that can. But it doesn't happen without a heart for God that is willing to gut it out in prayer, grow through tough times, and wait for love to be resurrected. We have to go through the pain to get to the joy.

You have to decide if you want your marriage to work, and if you want it badly enough to do whatever is necessary, within healthy parameters, to see it happen. *You* have to believe the part of your relationship that has been eaten away by pain, indifference, and selfishness can be restored. *You* have to trust that what has swarmed over you, such as abuse, death of a child, infidelity, poverty, loss, catastrophic illness, or accident, can be relieved of its death grip. *You* have to determine that everything consuming you and your husband, such as workaholism, alcoholism, drug abuse, or depression, can be destroyed. *You* have to know that whatever has crept into your relationship so silently and stealthily as to not even be perceived as a threat until it is clearly present – such as making idols of your career, your dreams, your kids, or your selfish desires – can be removed. *You* have to trust that God is big enough to accomplish all this and more.

If you wake up one morning with a stranger in your bed and it's your husband, if you experience a silent withdrawal from one another's lives that severs all emotional connection, if you sense a relentless draining away of love and hope, if your relationship is in so bottomless a pit of hurt and anger that every day sends you deeper into despair, if every word spoken drives a wedge further between you until it becomes an impenetrable barrier keeping you miles apart, be assured that none of the above is God's will for your marriage. God's will is to break down all these barriers and lift you out of that pit. He can heal the wounds and put love back in your heart. Nothing and no one else can.

But you have to rise up and say, 'Lord, I pray for an end to this conflict and a breaking of the hold strife has on us. Take away the hurt and the armor we've put up to protect ourselves. Lift us out of the pit of unforgiveness. Speak through us so that our words reflect Your love, peace, and reconciliation. Tear down this wall between us and teach us how to walk through it. Enable us to rise up from this paralysis and move into the healing and wholeness You have for us.'

Don't write off the marriage. Ask God to give you a new husband. He is able to take the one you have and make him a new creation in Christ. Husbands and wives are not destined to fight, emotionally disconnect, live in marital deadness, be miserable, or divorce. We have God's power on our side. We don't have to leave our marriages to chance. We can fight for them in prayer and not give up, because as long as we are praying, there is hope. With God, nothing is ever as dead as it seems. Not even your own feelings.

What About Me? I Need Prayer, Too

It's natural to enter into this prayer venture wondering if your husband will ever be praying for you in the same way you're praying for him. While that would certainly be great, don't count on it. Praying for your husband will be an act of unselfish, unconditional love and sacrifice on your part. You must be willing to make this commitment knowing it is quite possible – even highly probable – that he will never pray for you in the same way. In some cases, he may not pray for you at all. You can ask him to, and you can pray for him to pray for you, but you can't demand it of him. Regardless, whether he does or doesn't is not your concern, it's God's. So release him from that obligation. If he doesn't pray for you, it's *his* loss more than yours anyway. Your happiness and fulfillment will not ride on whether he prays, it will depend on your own relationship with the Lord. Yes, wives need prayer, too. But I'm convinced we should not depend on our husbands to be the sole providers of it. In fact, looking to your husband to be your dedicated prayer partner could be a setup for failure and disappointment for both of you.

I learned that the best thing for our marriage was for me to have women prayer partners with whom I prayed every week. I now believe this is vital for any marriage. If you can find two or more strong, faith-filled women whom you thoroughly trust, and with whom you can share the longings of your heart, set up a weekly prayer time. It will change your life. This doesn't mean you have to tell your prayer partners everything about your husband or expose the private details of his life. The purpose is to ask God to make *your* heart right, show *you* how to be a good wife, share the burdens of *your* soul, and seek God's blessing on your husband.

Of course, if there is an issue with serious consequences, and you can trust your prayer partners with the confidential nature of your request, by all means share it. I've seen many marriages end in separation or divorce because people were too prideful or afraid to share their problems with someone who could pray for them. They go along putting up a good front and suddenly one day the marriage is over. Be sure to stress the confidential nature of what you're sharing with your prayer partners, but don't throw away the marriage because you're hesitant to pray about it with others. If you have a prayer partner who can't keep a confidence, find someone else with more wisdom, sensitivity, and spiritual maturity.

Even without prayer partners or a praying husband, when you pray fervently you'll see things happen. *Before* your prayers are answered there will be blessings from God that will come to you simply because you are praying. That's because you will have spent time in the presence of God, where all lasting transformation begins.

One Prayer at a Time

Don't be overwhelmed by the many ways there are to pray for your husband. It's not necessary to do it all in one day, one week, or even a month. Let the suggestions in this book be a guide and then pray as the Holy Spirit leads you. Where there are tough issues and you need a dynamic breakthrough, fasting will make your prayers more effective. Also, praying Scripture over your husband is powerful. That's what I have done in the prayers at the end of each chapter, wherever you see a Scripture reference.

Above all, don't give place to impatience. Seeing answers to your prayers can take time, especially if your marriage is deeply wounded or strained. Be patient to persevere and wait for God to heal. Keep in mind that you are both imperfect people. Only the Lord is perfect. Look to God as the source of all you want to see happen in your marriage, and don't worry about *how* it will happen. It's your responsibility to pray. It's God's job to answer. Leave it in *His* hands.

Cooking Up Worship

David E. Flavell

Just like a well-planned menu, what we share in church together should be interesting, wholesome, nourishing and do everyone good. Now we all know that peoples' taste in food can differ. The same is true for styles of worship.

Do you feel called to lead worship but lack the confidence and expertise to volunteer? Then *Cooking Up Worship* is for you. Experienced laity and clergy may pick up some useful tips too. Everything is covered in practical detail – from setting the scene, content, music, to special services. There are even some real recipes.

To worship is to give worth, to give glory to God. This book will do just that.

Bon appetit!

Kevin Mayhew
ISBN: 1-8400-3375-4

Price: £9.99

Jardin's Principle

Jardin – who may have been a French Catholic, or a Scottish Presbyterian, nobody is quite sure – says that any given problem can be looked at in three ways:

  (a) Simplistic (b) Complex (c) Simple but profound

Thus, for a restaurant, the aim can be stated in three ways, as follows:

(a) We should make more profit

(b) We should aim to increase our market share by three points in the next year, whilst concentrating on cutting capital input by one fifth, and also maximising menu efficiency and so on

(c) We should aim to give our customers what they really want.

Answer (a) is simplistic – of course we want to make more profit. Answer (b) is complex and will run to dozens of pages. Answer (c) is simple, but profound. It is a very easy concept to get across, but in another way it raises more questions than it answers. How do we give our customers what they really want? How do we find out? How do we deliver? How do we get everybody working in the restaurant to take responsibility for this? And there are many more questions like this.

But doesn't this ring a bell for Christians? Isn't there somebody we know who, when asked complex theological questions, came back with simple but profound answers which raised a whole new set of questions? It should come as no surprise to us that Jesus was a great Jardinist, long before the *Principle* was thought of.

Take Luke Chapter 10, the story of the Good Samaritan:

- The original question is 'Teacher, what must I do to inherit eternal life?'
- Jesus asks, 'What does the Law say?'
- To which the answer comes: 'Love the Lord your God with all your heart, and with all your soul, with all your strength and with all your mind; and your neighbour as yourself.'
- Jesus says, 'That is the right answer'.

Now the 'love your neighbour as yourself' bit is simple but profound. It's a very deep subject upon which many a sermon has been preached. Unfortunately, the lawyer takes it as being simplistic. After all, a lawyer's job is to make simple things complex. He tries for a more intricate answer. The response he gets is one of the greatest stories in literature, that of the Good Samaritan, which is at once simple but profound, and to which there is no answer. So Jesus leads the lawyer beyond the simplistic and the complicated and into the simple but profound.

When we look at worship today, we have not made the same step forward. The great argument at present is between choruses and hymns. One side says 'Choruses are puerile – the words are childish'. In other words choruses are too simplistic. The other side says 'Hymns are boring – they're too slow and the words are old-fashioned and incomprehensible'. In other words hymns are too complex.

The argument is stuck at the stage of simplistic worship versus complex worship. Neither is adequate. To make a difference to people, what we really need is to provide *simple but profound* worship. That is your task. May this book show you how.

Chapter 1

Laying the Table
Setting the Scene

Preparing an act of worship is like preparing a meal. Why?
Because:

- whatever you do, it will never be to everybody's taste
- you mix together various ingredients to make the whole
- good quality ingredients make for a good quality meal
- some ingredients blend better together than others
- some people will be the equivalent of militant vegans and will be offended if you include something they don't like
- some people are obsessive about etiquette and liable to go berserk if you don't do everything in what they consider to be the right order and the right way
- some people only like the sweet bits and aren't bothered about how nourishing the food is
- some people go from place to place sampling the products until they are satisfied
- some people enjoy complaining, no matter how good it is
- what really counts is not how clever you are, but how good it tastes

- the best cooks sometimes have disasters
- it's easier to eat than to cook

Maybe you can work out some more comparisons of your own!

What are We Getting at the Moment?

What the institutional church tends to offer is 'Sunday roast'. It is the same thing each week, with the same set courses, the same approach, the same structure. A prevailing attitude is that if people don't like this approach, then they jolly well ought to: 'It was good enough for the last century, so it's good enough now. If people don't come to church, then it's their own fault. We should be grateful for what we get, no matter how bad it is. For what we are about to receive, may the Lord *make* us truly thankful. What we offer is right. And if you don't like paternalism, then you don't know what's good for you, sonny.'

That's fine for the ever-diminishing bunch who like it, but what about the rest of us?

In the 'golden age' of yesteryear, the whole family sat down together and ate Sunday lunch in the traditional way. Mum would prepare a starter, a main course and a pudding followed by coffee. Dad and the kids would volunteer to wash up and afterwards everybody would sit down to talk or watch the film on TV while Dad fell asleep and snored loudly.

In the same way, at Sunday worship, the Church family would come together in the traditional manner. The minister would prepare the service with a nice word for the children, who would then go off to Sunday school. He would then read the Bible and give his sermon while Dad fell asleep and snored loudly until Mum prodded him. There would be nice hymns and a touching benediction. The congregation would express their thanks and go home to the traditional Sunday lunch.

This world has disappeared, but has the Church really noticed? Only a small minority of households sit down to Sunday roast today. Only a small minority of households come to church today. *These facts are linked.* Just as society has changed its eating habits, so it has changed its worship habits. Sunday is now a day just like Saturday.

Yet people still need to worship. The spiritual dimension has not vanished from life. The mainstream church is not providing the answer; there is a resistance to change for fear of 'upsetting somebody'.

Two Examples of Change

In the North East of England, in Easington Village, the traditional way of worship had led to just six elderly people meeting together on a Sunday. By changing the way of doing things and letting the people lead the worship, the average weekly attendance grew to over forty adults within six months.

On Merseyside, the Liverpool Central Hall closed in 1994 and was sold to property developers because it had only a handful of worshippers. In 1998 a new Church was started in the upper room of a pub in Liverpool city centre. The services were led by a team who used attractive and relevant ways of worshipping, and numbers rocketed. (See Chapter 10 for more details.)

Seven Meals that Jesus Shared

- Wedding at Cana John 2:1–11
- Feeding of the Five Thousand Mark 6:30–44
- Dinner with Simon the Pharisee Luke 7:36–50
- Meal with Mary and Martha Luke 10:38–42
- Tea with Zacchaeus Luke 19:1–10
- The Last Supper Mark 14:17–25
- Breakfast in Galilee John 21:9–14

Spiritual Hunger

There is a need for change because the nation is starving. If the Church is not feeding people's spiritual hunger, *then it ought to be*. There is still a need for simple but profound worship, and there are too many churches where that need is not being met. Too many leaders in the Church want the congregation to accept what they are given, rather than to learn to worship for themselves.

This is not what the Church is supposed to be about. The Church is better at being true to itself when it follows the way of Jesus. He put himself out for those who found the religion of the day hard to understand. He said that he had not come to call the righteous, but sinners. He went to the outcasts of society, and ate with them in *their* way, in *their* homes. The Church expects outsiders to learn the Church way of doing things before they can be accepted.

People should feel at home in church. They should be allowed to be themselves in church. Instead they have to pretend to enjoy what they are given.

What Need to be Done?

There is no standard meal that everybody will eat this Sunday lunchtime. There does not have to be a standard form of worship that every church has to provide this Sunday. There are no 'norms' in worship, no objective standards that are laid down in Scripture. Instead, leaders of worship make their own choices.

They often choose the traditional way, because that seems to be the easiest. But the traditional way is not working for the vast majority of the population who do not come to church, and I would assert that it is not working for a large number of people who *do* come to church and come out of a sense of duty.

How many times do people leave church thinking, 'That was all very nice, but completely irrelevant to me'? *I'm afraid it is far too many times.*

How many people really enjoy the style of their worship every week and how many would like more variety, more quality, more choice?

There needs to be a complete change in attitude if the Church is to provide meaningful worship in today's world. The crucial thing is that people are fed. *How* they are fed is less important. There is no one 'correct' way to share a meal. Sometimes simple food with friends, where everybody helps themselves from the packet, is better than a meal at a sophisticated restaurant where you're not quite sure if you're following the right etiquette. Simple, informal worship can be far better than an elaborate service where nobody knows whether they are following the protocol or not.

The one thing that *is* essential for a meal is food. Without food there is no meal. With food, any kind of food, a meal can be prepared. Traditionalists will demand that lamb cannot be served without mint sauce. Formalists will direct that the port must be passed to the left and that gentlemen shall be properly dressed. But what we think of as essentials are culturally conditioned. What we think of as normal, may only be normal to us. For instance, one third of the world eats with its fingers, one third eats with chopsticks and only one third eats with cutlery. But if you started eating a meal with your fingers at home in Britain, your mother would give you a lecture about your table manners.

The one element that *is* essential for Christian worship is Jesus Christ. He said, 'For where two or three are gathered together in my name, there am I in the midst of them' (Matthew 18:20). With his presence among us, we are able to worship. Traditionalists will demand that we cannot have hymns without an organ. Formalists will direct that there must be a pulpit and that gentlemen shall be properly dressed. But some people will be worshipping this day in a prison cell, with nothing but the presence of Jesus Christ. And that is still worship.

Our ideas of Christianity are dominated by our experience of Western churches. If you suddenly started singing like they do in the Armenian Church (which sounds to the uneducated ear like a sort of Middle-Eastern melodic wail), the choir director would suggest you didn't come back again. Different traditions have different ingredients of worship. Thus *no set of ingredients is objectively right or wrong*; it all depends on local tastes. The diverse nature of Christian worship is a strength, not a weakness.

- There can be worship without hymns.
- There can be worship without Bible readings.

Seven Ways to Intimidate Dinner Guests

- Give them lots of cutlery and expect them to know what to use and when
- Wear formal dress and stare at them when they don't
- Stand up and sit down unexpectedly for special toasts
- Assume they know all about a subject and talk about it for ages
- Give them a meal full of gristle and expect them to say they've enjoyed it
- Ignore them completely and talk to your other friends
- Ask them to bring their children with them and then complain when they make a noise

You wouldn't do that to your dinner guests. Would you?

Seven Ways to Intimidate Worship Guests

- Give them lots of books and expect them to know what to use and when
- Wear formal dress and stare at them when they don't
- Stand up and sit down unexpectedly for hymns, prayers and readings
- Assume they know all about a subject and give a sermon about it for ages
- Give them a service full of dreary hymns and expect them to say they've enjoyed it
- Ignore them completely and talk to your other friends
- Ask them to bring their children with them and then complain when they make a noise

The Church isn't like this at all. Is it?

- There can be worship without prayer.
- There can be worship without books.
- There can be worship without a sermon.
- There can be worship without a building.
- There can be worship without a minister.
- There can be worship without a collection.
- Christians can worship together in silence, in the middle of nowhere.

The traditional Sunday service is *not* the only way to worship.

Turning Points

Vaughan Roberts

Are you looking for meaning in your life, or want to know how you fit into the grand scheme of things?

In today's throwaway society, does history help us make sense of the big questions we face? Vaughan Roberts tackles these questions and others as he looks at what the Bible presents as the 'turning points' in history, from creation to the end of the world.

Vaughan faced his own turning point at the age of eighteen when he began to follow Jesus. Now Rector of St Ebbe's Church, Oxford he has his finger on the pulse of today's culture. Here he uses his gift of thoughtful persuasion to pass on to others the true meaning of life.

OM Publishing
ISBN: 1-8507-8336-5

Price: £5.99

6

The Day Death Died[1]

Three people die every second, 180 every minute, almost 11,000 every hour, about 260,000 every day and 95 million a year.[2] It has been described as the ultimate statistic: one in one dies. But despite its inevitability, very few of us ever talk about death. The Victorians had a morbid fascination with the subject but were very coy when it came to sexuality. We are the exact opposite. Sex is everywhere, but we keep death hidden as much as possible. Someone has put it well: "If the nineteenth century tried to conceal the facts of life, the twentieth tries to conceal the facts of death." We say, "She has kicked the bucket", "He has passed away", but hardly ever, "He's dead" – that sounds too blunt, too final. In the Middle Ages it was not unusual for prominent people to have a skull on their desks as a "*memento mori*" – a reminder of their mortality. We are very different today. The undertaker who is reported to have signed his letters, "Yours eventually" and said, "See you soon" when saying goodbye, will not have been popular. We prefer to hide death away in morgues and crematoria. Many of us have never seen a dead body. On the few occasions when we are forced to face death we tend to make light of it and pretend that it is not that bad after all. An advert for the Rosewood Memorial Park at Tidewater, West Virginia, said, "Now you can enjoy dying. Call today for information about clean, dry, ventilated entombment at special pre-construction prices!"[3]

This awkwardness concerning death reveals a deep-rooted fear. Peter Hall, the theatre director, said recently, "I do think about death every day and always have done."[4] Woody Allen famously said once: "It's not that I'm afraid to die; I just don't want to be around when it happens." The joke could not disguise the fear. In one interview he said: "The fundamental thing behind all motivation and all activity is the constant struggle against annihilation and death. It is absolutely stupefying in its terror, and it renders anyone's accomplishments meaningless." We are afraid not simply of the process of death and the uncertainty that lies beyond but also of its implications. Allen was surely right. If death is the end, then our few fleeting years on earth will be soon forgotten. It will not be long before no one will remember us at all. All that we strove for is rendered "meaningless". H.G. Wells saw that clearly: "If there is no afterlife, then life is just a sick joke, braying across the centuries."

Perhaps that explains the rise in the belief in reincarnation – anything is better than extinction. David Icke told the world in his book *Truth Vibrations* that he had first appeared on earth at the start of the Atlantis civilization. Since then, in the course of a long series of reincarnations, he was married in ancient Greece to a woman called Lucy, became the brother of the seventeenth-century philosopher Francis Bacon, was one of Napoleon's generals and a North American Indian chief. But what evidence is there for such wild claims?

Others prefer to put their faith in science. An increasing

number of people are paying up to £60,000 to practitioners of "cryonics". The blood is drained from the corpse which is then filled with freezer fluid, encased in aluminium and suspended in a bath of liquid nitrogen. The hope is that a cure will be found for the disease that causes death which will enable life to be resumed after the body has been thawed.[5] It is a large investment for a very slim chance of a return.

This widespread fear of death is not surprising. The Bible teaches that it is an enemy – an alien intruder which was not part of God's original plan for the perfect world that he made. Human beings were not designed to die – death only entered the world after the Fall. You will remember that God told Adam and Eve that they could eat of any tree in the Garden of Eden except the tree of the knowledge of good and evil. The command came with a warning: "If you eat of it you will surely die."[6] It happened just as God had said. Once the first humans had eaten of the forbidden fruit God banished them from his presence and prevented them from returning to the tree of life. The symbolism is powerful. Death is the result of human rebellion against God. From now on human beings would be mortal. As the apostle Paul put it in the New Testament: "The wages of sin is death".[7]

We have seen in the last two chapters that the Bible proclaims Jesus to be the great rescuer who has come from God. He came to undo the effects of the Fall and to introduce the kingdom of God, in which everything is restored to its perfection and the world is once again as it was designed to be. To make that possible he had to deal with the fundamental problem – our sin and God's righteous anger against it. That he achieved by his death on the cross. But how can we be sure that the death of one man all those years ago really was the key turning point of history? Why should we believe that he achieved a great victory there which changes everything? The Bible's answer is to point us to the resurrection of Jesus from the dead. Death, the great sign of the judgement of God which spoils this world, has been defeated. We need not fear it any more; instead we can have hope as we face the future. And that hope is not based on mere wishful thinking; it is firmly rooted in an historical event: the first Easter Day – the day death died.

The Christian claim

Every year *Varsity* and *Cherwell*, the university newspapers of Oxford and Cambridge, conduct joint surveys. The results in 1995 reached the front page of *The Independent*: "Students say the person they most admire is Christ and their favourite book is the Bible. Going to church rates among their favourite activities along with drinking, socialising and listening to music." Jim Murphy, President of the National Union of Students, commented that the newly revealed popularity of Jesus and the Bible was "bizarre". "I am surprised and shocked. I have never heard anything like it before".[8] The survey the following year showed the same result. Jesus topped the poll for favourite hero or heroine, beating such luminaries as Margaret Thatcher, Kurt Cobain, Richard Dawkins and Dylan from *The Magic Roundabout*. He lived and died nearly 2000 years ago and yet still he has a huge impact on our world – Jesus lives on.

A recent *Sunday Times* article about Freddie Mercury ended with these words: "So, Freddie is not dead. He may not have been spotted in as many supermarkets as Elvis, but his fans are just as reluctant to let him go. Pop stars are immortal because they provide the soundtrack for other peoples' lives."[9] Many famous figures from history live on in that sense – their influence continues. But the Christian claim is that Jesus does not just live on in the minds of his followers. He really is alive. He died but then he was raised from the dead, never to die again. That is why, down the ages, Christians have been able to say they know him as a living presence in their lives.

It had been an excellent first week of our family holiday in the Dordogne in southern France. My parents, twin sister and I had all got on well – there was remarkably little tension. But then my elder sister arrived. We picked her up from the train station and it was as we were returning to the camp site that she said it: "You aren't real Christians you know." She had been an earnest Christian since starting at university and we had talked before about her faith but she had never been as blunt as this. I was livid and started shouting at her. How dare she suggest that we were not Christians? After all, we lived pretty decent lives compared to many people and we even went to church fairly regularly. What arrogance to imply that she was a Christian and we were not! The rest of the journey passed in an awkward silence. I hardly spoke to her for the rest of the week – the holiday had been spoilt. The Sunday after we returned home she decided that she wanted to go to a church in the local town which had been recommended to her and she asked me to drive her. It was the last thing I wanted to do but my mother pointed out that I had been so beastly to her over the previous few days that it was the least I could do and it might shut her up.

I felt uncomfortable throughout the whole service but I was struck by what I saw and heard. The minister began by announcing some sad news. A child, whose parents were church members, had been killed in a bicycle accident the previous day. Another couple stood up to pray for this family. Before they began they said that something very similar had happened to them a few years before. They had lost a much-loved child and were devastated, but they spoke movingly about how Jesus had been very close to them in their grief and had helped them through. It was then that I realized that my sister had been absolutely right, even if she had not been tactful. Here were people who talked of a personal relationship with Jesus and of him making a difference in their lives, even in painful circumstances. They claimed to know him. I knew nothing of that. My Christianity was limited to going to church from time to time and trying to live a decent life. It was then that I resolved to look into the Christian faith for myself and make my own decision about it, one way or the other. I began by reading one of the New Testament gospels. As I did so I found myself being drawn very strongly to the person of Jesus. He spoke to me not as a voice from the dead but as a living presence. I became convinced that he was alive and that he was calling me to follow him. I have been doing so for fifteen years now and I am as convinced now as I was then that Jesus is alive – he has changed my life. Countless Christians could say the same.

The evidence for the resurrection

It is all very well to talk of Christian experience but could we not be deluded? People believe all sorts of strange things with great conviction but that does not make them true. Is there any historical evidence for the resurrection? Yes there is. I will focus on just two facts.

1: The tomb was empty

Jesus died on a Friday. The next day was the Jewish Sabbath which was strictly observed by the Jews as a day of rest, so it was on the Sunday that some women went to the tomb to attend to Jesus' body and put spices on it. When they arrived they found that the body had disappeared. At least five disciples are recorded as having witnessed the strange scene. The linen cloths which had been wrapped round the body were still there, undisturbed, but there was nothing inside them. What happened to that body? A number of suggestions have been made.

Grave robbers stole it
- But why would they have picked on the only tomb in Jerusalem that was guarded? And why take the one thing that was worthless, the body, and leave the cloths and the spices, the only items of any value in that tomb? There was no anatomy department in Jerusalem desperate for bodies to dissect. That body would have been useless to them.

The women went to the wrong tomb
- But Mark's gospel tells us quite specifically that they had seen where he had been buried.[10] And is it not highly unlikely that the reports of Jesus' resurrection would have been allowed to persist without someone going to the correct tomb and pointing out that the body was still there?

The Roman authorities stole the body
- No doubt they knew that Jesus had said that he would rise again after his death, so perhaps they took the body into safe keeping to prevent any of his disciples stealing

it and then claiming that he had risen? That would have prevented any chance of another troublesome religious cult emerging. But if they had done that why did they not produce the body when news of the resurrection began to spread? That would have killed the rumours stone dead.

The disciples stole it

• They had staked their lives on their belief that Jesus was the Messiah. No doubt their parents had said that it was just a phase they were going through and their friends had laughed at their religious fervour. And when Jesus died they realized that they had indeed been fools. They could not face owning up and going back home and saying, "Mum, Dad, you were right all along – he was a fraud", so they decided to pretend that he had risen from the dead. They stole the body, hid it and then started proclaiming that he was the risen Messiah. But does that really make sense? Even the most basic knowledge of human psychology would tell you that they really believed that he was alive. Why else would they have gone to such great efforts to spread the news about him, to the extent that they were often martyred for their faith? People may die for what is not true, but would they really have died for what they *knew* was not true – because they had invented it?

2: Jesus appeared to his followers

Over a period of six weeks Jesus appeared to different groups of his followers on at least ten occasions. At one time he was seen by 500 people at once. Paul tells us that most of them were still alive as he wrote – in other words, those who did not believe him could go and ask them.[11] They were not naïve gullible individuals who found it easy to believe that a dead man had come back to life; it was just that there was no other explanation. Thomas, the sceptic, had not been present when Jesus appeared to the other disciples. He would not believe what they told him: "Unless I see the nail marks in his hands and put my finger where the nails were, and put my hand into his side, I will not believe it." A week later Jesus came again. He said to Thomas, "Put your finger here; see my hands. Reach out your hand and put it into my side. Stop doubting and believe." Thomas simply replied, "My Lord and my God."[12]

These extraordinary events were not invented – I have argued already that it is clear that the first Christians were convinced that Jesus had risen. What possible explanations are there?

Jesus had not died

- He looked dead, so the soldiers took him down from the cross and put him in the tomb. But once there, the cool air revived him; he pushed the stone away from the entrance and escaped. It was this revived Jesus, rather than the risen Jesus, that the disciples saw. But is that really plausible? Is it possible that a man who had been flogged, hung on a cross for six hours, lost consciousness and been in a tomb for three days without food or medical help, could have revived? And even if he had done so, it is hardly likely that he could have persuaded anyone that he had conquered death – he would have been barely alive.

The disciples hallucinated

- But hallucinations almost always come to those who are longing for something to happen – as a wish-fulfillment.

The disciples, by their own admission, had not been expecting the resurrection. And hallucinations are very individual – not shared in every detail by groups, as in the New Testament accounts. Furthermore, the risen Jesus could be seen, heard and touched. He had detailed conversations with people. He even ate some fish!

Jesus had indeed risen from the dead

- As I examined the evidence for the resurrection for the first time, I came to see that it was far easier to believe that Jesus had risen than to believe the alternatives – it is amazing what you have to believe to not believe. All the evidence supports the claims of those first disciples. How else can one explain the astonishing change in them? After Jesus was arrested they were dejected and close to despair. They had hoped that he was the Messiah, but now all their dreams had been dashed as they had seen him die a humiliating death. They were petrified that the next knock on the door would be the Roman authorities arresting them for following Jesus. But something happened to change this pathetic rabble into men of such power that they turned the world upside down by their preaching. And then there was Saul, a vicious opponent of the newly flourishing Christian movement. What changed him into the great apostle Paul who became the greatest of the early Christian preachers? It was the fact of the resurrection. "Last of all", he wrote, "he appeared to me."[13]

The consequences of the resurrection

The resurrection is another of the great turning points of history. It has enormous repercussions for us and for our world. We will consider two.

1: *Jesus really is the promised Messiah*

18 June 1815 is one of the most significant dates in British history – the day on which Wellington faced Napoleon at Waterloo. The future of the nation was at stake. People up and down the country were on tenterhooks – everyone was waiting to hear what had happened. One of the main lookout posts was the roof of Winchester Cathedral, from where the channel could just be seen. At last the signal ships came into view. A severe fog almost prevented the signal from being visible. But before the mist finally came down, the essentials of the message could just be made out: "WELLINGTON DEFEATED." The worst had happened, and the depressing news began to spread from beacon to beacon. A few hours later, the fog lifted, and only then could the full message be seen: "WELLINGTON DEFEATED THE FRENCH."

It would be hard to find a more pathetic picture of weakness than Jesus on the cross. He did not look like the great Messiah that he had declared himself to be. His miracles had suggested that he might indeed have been the mighty king promised by the prophets, but his death seemed to put an end to that idea. The paintings sanitize the scene, but make no mistake – it was not pretty. It was full of blood and tears and sweat. Every breath Jesus took sent the pain stabbing through his body as he had to lift himself up on the nails. And all the time he was surrounded by a jeering mob who were enjoying the spectacle. No doubt they laughed at the crown of thorns on his head and the mocking sign above him: "The King of the Jews." Some king! As far as they were concerned, the message of the cross was crystal clear: "JESUS DEFEATED". But how wrong they were. That twisted, agonized figure was and is the Lord of life, and in his death he was achieving the greatest victory the world has ever seen. That victory was only proclaimed two days later when, on the first Easter Sunday, he rose from the dead. Then, at last, could the full message be seen: "JESUS DEFEATED THE GRAVE." Jesus was not just a religious teacher; he was and is the mighty, victorious Messiah. The resurrection reveals the true identity of Jesus. As Paul wrote to some Christians in Rome, "He was declared with power to be the Son of God, by his resurrection from the dead."[14] His friends buried him in a tomb, but God raised him to a throne. It was the great vindication of all that he had said about himself. Once we recognize the truth of the resurrection we should all use the words of Thomas: "My Lord and my God."

2: Jesus really is introducing the new age

The hope held out by the prophets was nothing less than the transformation of everything. When the Messiah came he would bring an end to this present world, spoilt by our rebellion against God, and introduce a new age, the kingdom of God, in which everything is restored to its perfection – life as it was meant to be. On the cross Jesus achieved the victory against God's enemies that made that possible. But that victory was not evident until the resurrection. The fact that Jesus rose from the dead proved that death had indeed been conquered – Jesus defeated the grave.

"Death has been swallowed up in victory. Where, O death, is your victory? Where, O death, is your sting?"[15] The fact that Jesus defeated death does not simply show that he is the Messiah; it also proves that he is able to introduce the new age that the prophets had promised. The resurrection marked the beginning of that new age. It proved that there was life beyond death.

For many years Europeans believed that there was no land to the west of Portugal. There was a large plaque in the port of Lisbon which simply said: "Ne plus ultra" – "Nothing beyond this". But, as you know from your history at school, "In fourteen hundred and ninety-two, Columbus sailed the ocean blue" and discovered America. When he returned to Portugal the plaque was changed. It now read: "Plus ultra" – "There *is* more beyond this".

Before the resurrection there was no hope of anything beyond death. This world was trapped "in bondage to decay."[16] Sin led inevitably to death and eternal separation from God, and there was nothing that could be done about it. But Jesus changed all that. On the cross he took the penalty for sin upon himself and, as a result, the power of death was broken. It was now possible for God to introduce the new age, marked not by death but by life – eternal life in relationship with him. It is the resurrection that proclaims that possibility: "Plus ultra" – "There is more beyond this".

The new age has not been fully introduced yet, but the process which will lead in time to the new creation has begun with the resurrection. C.S. Lewis expressed this truth powerfully in one of his essays:

To be sure, it feels wintry enough still: but often in the very early spring it feels like that. 2000 years are only a day or two by this scale. A man really ought to say 'the resurrection happened' in the same spirit in which he says 'I saw a crocus yesterday'. The spring comes slowly down this way; but the great thing is that the corner has been turned.[17]

Elsewhere he writes: "He has forced open a door that has been locked since the death of the first man. He has met, fought and beaten the King of Death. Everything is different because he has done so. This is the beginning of the new creation. A new chapter in cosmic history has opened."[18]

The New Testament teaches that, because Jesus has defeated death, all those who trust in him can share in his victory. They can die with the confidence that death is not the end. There is life beyond the grave. That explains the remarkable assurance and peace that so many Christians have shown in their final days on earth. John Rogers was burnt for his faith in 1555. The French ambassador witnessed the scene. He said later that Rogers had walked to his death "as if he was walking to his wedding." I think of Mark Ruston, a vicar in Cambridge for many years, who had a deep impact on the lives of many undergraduates, including mine. He had retired and knew that he was dying of cancer. It would have been easy to dwell on the past, but he had his eyes fixed firmly on the future and he was able to say: "The best is yet to come". The twinkle in his eyes as he said those words confirmed to me that he really believed them. He wrote to a friend a month before he died: "I cannot honestly say that I look forward to the last bit of the journey, but beyond that I know that I shall see Christ, and what could compare with that?"

Bertrand Russell once said that Christian optimism about the future life is "built on the ground that fairy tales are pleasant".[19] Is that all that the hope of John Rogers,

A History of the World

The story so far:

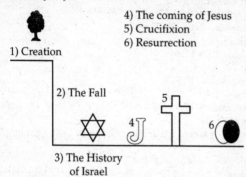

1) Creation

4) The coming of Jesus
5) Crucifixion
6) Resurrection

2) The Fall

3) The History
of Israel

Mark Ruston, and countless other Christians consists of? Were they simply clutching at straws? No – their confidence was built on solid ground. Peter, one of the first disciples, wrote: "Praise be to the God and Father of our Lord Jesus Christ, who in his great mercy has given us new birth into a living hope, through the resurrection of Jesus Christ from the dead."[20] It is the fact of the resurrection that is the foundation of Christian hope. The decisive battle has been won; it is now only a matter of time before the full fruits of that victory are enjoyed forever.

Notes

[1] The title of a book on the resurrection by Michael Green (IVP, 1982).

[2] John Blanchard, *Whatever Happened to Hell?*, (Evangelical Press, 1993) 46.

[3] David Watson, *Is Anyone There?*, (IVP, 1979) 65.

[4] *The Sunday Times*, 1-3-92.

[5] Blanchard, *Whatever Happened to Hell?*, 47.

[6] Genesis 2:17.

[7] Romans 6:23.

[8] *The Independent*, 11-12-95.

[9] *The Sunday Times*, 17-11-96.

[10] Mark 15:47.

[11] 1 Corinthians 15:6.

[12] John 20:25–28.

[13] 1 Corinthians 15:8.

[14] Romans 1:4.

[15] 1 Corinthians 15:54–55.

[16] Romans 8:21.

[17] From "The Grand Miracle" in *God in the Dock*, (Fount, 1998) 58.

[18] From *Miracles*, (Fontana, 1947) 149.

[19] Quoted in Michael Green, *The Empty Cross of Jesus*, (Hodder, 1984) 132.

[20] 1 Peter 1:3.

The Sixty Minute Mother

Rob Parsons

In our busy lives what can we learn in **one** hour that will have lasting benefit? Those familiar with Rob Parsons' *Sixty Minute* series will be sure to answer 'Lots!'

Now Rob turns his considerable wit and wisdom to the subject of motherhood.

We meet 'ordinary mums' who stay at home and 'super mums' who appear to have it all – each share their experiences and from each we can learn valuable lessons and some surprising spiritual insights.

Interspersed with the anecdotes you'll find the Parsons' unique brand of *Sixty Second Wisdom*.

Take a break with *The Sixty Minute Mother*.

Hodder & Stoughton
ISBN: 0-3406-3061-2

Price: £6.99

3

When a Mother Accepts

'What is the greatest gift a mother can give a child?' That was the question asked of four hundred women at a recent seminar. The most common reply by a long way, was 'love'.

I'm not at all sure it is the right answer. If it is, then we should be pleased, for although most of us have critics, enemies, and those who find us just plain irritating, our mothers love us. One of the most embarrassing moments of my life occurred at 10.30 on a winter's morning when I was thirty-nine years old. At that time I was a senior partner in a legal practice and had a rather pompous and crusty bank manager as a passenger in my car. As we made our way along a busy street I saw my mother shopping. She would have been almost eighty then and was struggling with a large bag in the rain. 'That's my mother over there', I said to my passenger. 'We're very near her home; is it all right if we give her a lift?' For the first time that week the bank manager said 'Yes'.

My dear old mother clambered into the back seat and we began to make our way to the street where she lived. A few moments passed in silence and then she leant forward, tapped the banker on the shoulder, pointed at me, and said to him, 'Don't you think he's lovely?' He replied, 'Very nice indeed, Mrs Parsons.'

So if it is not love that is the greatest gift, what can it possibly be? I am convinced it is – acceptance. If a child does not feel accepted by his or her mother, it is almost impossible for them to feel loved by her.

We hear a great deal these days about 'peer pressure' with regard to raising children and it is true that this dwarfs the power of parental influence for many children, especially in the teenage years. But, in truth, peer pressure is a phenomenon that affects us all – we crave to be accepted. What else could make millions of us eat rabbit food, and torture ourselves on treadmills, or have plastic surgeons yank, stretch and redistribute vast areas of our skin so that we look younger? Somebody has convinced us that youth and a certain style of beauty are the things that make us acceptable, and what we want, almost as much as life itself, is to be accepted.

One of the greatest services we can do for our children is to send them into adulthood believing that at least their parents accept them for who they are. In the next section we look at two ways in which children perceive whether or not they really are loved like that.

'I Accept the Way You Look'

One of the greatest pressures on children in modern society is the way they look. Amongst the most rampant diseases plaguing the young are the eating disorders of anorexia and bulimia. In one study two thousand girls from eleven to eighteen were asked, 'What would you most like to change about yourself if you could?' Fifty-nine per cent mentioned some aspect of their physical appearance, with only four per cent desiring greater ability. In another study, children were asked to complete the sentence, 'I wish I were . . .'. The majority of boys answered, 'Taller' and the girls, 'Smaller'.

We live in a world in which thin is beautiful. In the western world we forget this is a purely cultural phenomenon. A friend of mine went to Uganda. On showing some of the women a photograph of her family one of them said, 'Oh, your mother is beautiful – she is fat just like you.' If you've got a moment, browse through a local art gallery. Observe the paintings of women of a few hundred years ago; I guarantee there won't be a size fourteen in sight, never mind a size ten. These were large women – and thought of as beautiful. One woman put it well: 'Society always wants women to be the shape it's hardest for us to achieve. In Victorian times when good food was hard to come by, the fashionable shape was ":well-rounded". Now, with an abundance of foods, not to mention Mars bars, they want us to look like stick-insects.'

Kids aren't stupid; they know that ugly girls don't get on the front covers of teen magazines or unattractive boys adorn the inside pages. But way before that they have been introduced to the world of 'beautiful baby' competitions. One of the saddest sights imaginable must be that of adults who should know better, solemnly gazing into pram after pram and judging who is or who is not a 'beautiful baby'. What, for goodness sake, does a beautiful baby look like? And because of that pressure countless mothers who will give birth today will, over the coming weeks, feel disappointed with the way their baby looks. They wanted a cuddly, rounded, rosy-cheeked, smiling, angel. What they got looks like a cross between a drowned rat and a prune.

But here's the rub: as that baby grows she will assess from a million messages – some screamed at her from adverts, some whispered in school playgrounds and most unsaid – whether or not she is 'beautiful'. Unless that child is destined to be one of the few who meet the standard she will have to do battle with the world if she is to hold on to her self-esteem. She ought not to have to do battle in the home.

Not far from us lives a very attractive mum. This woman is slim, and looks ten years younger than her forty years. Her daughter is seventeen and a little over-weight. The other day the mother, in the hearing of some of her daughter's friends, said, 'You know, Ceri, I'm forty and I'm in better shape than you.' Does that mother love her daughter? Yes, she would probably die for her. Does she accept her? No.

Who is the Fairest of Them All?

It's amazing how early in life our children imbibe the idea that they must look a certain way to be acceptable. Take, for example, some well-known children's stories. Before you switch off let me assure you, I do not think we should re-write every fairy tale to make it politically correct. One of the funniest books published recently takes a sideways swipe at that philosophy. Here's a short example from a politically correct 'Red Riding Hood'.[2]

> The wolf said, 'You know my dear, it isn't safe for a little girl to walk through these woods alone'.
>
> Red Riding Hood said, 'I find your sexist remark offensive in the extreme, but I will ignore it because of your traditional status as an outcast from society, the stress of which has caused you to develop your

own, entirely valid, world view. Now, if you'll excuse me, I must be on my way'.

Red Riding Hood walked along the main path. But, because his status outside society had freed him from slavish adherence to linear, Western-style thought, the wolf knew a quicker route to Grandma's house . . .

But having laughed at that, just consider the role of beauty in some of these popular stories and what this may say to our kids. 'The Ugly Duckling' is a nice example. At first it looks promising – this little duckling who doesn't fit the mould and is ostracised. So how does our hero get over this? Is it by using other gifts to make his mark, or triumphing by sheer personality? No, he does it by – becoming beautiful. Inside the ugly duckling is a beautiful swan just waiting to emerge. How many kids have looked in the mirror each morning and wondered how long it will be before their swan shows up?

Or enter the world of Disney and 'Snow White and the Seven Dwarfs'. That story has a magic mirror in it. Not only does this mirror possess incredible powers, it allows you, once in a while, to ask it questions. Think of that. What question would you ask a magic mirror? Well, how about, 'Who is the fairest of them all?' We know none of the dwarfs are in the frame, but we needn't have worried, because our tall, slim, dark-haired beauty is ready to help – so long as we can stop her eating apples.

The list goes on – 'Sleeping Beauty', 'Beauty and the Beast' – but without doubt the best example is 'Cinderella'. Look at any child's illustrated book of this timeless story. In the beginning Cinderella looks dirty, unwashed, and her clothes certainly aren't designer. But there is no doubt that this woman is gorgeous. When the fairy godmother comes she doesn't give Cinders a face-lift – this kid doesn't need one – and you can bet your bottom dollar that the handsome prince wasn't bowled off his feet by the horses, or the coach, even if he did guess they were actually a bunch of mice and a pumpkin. And who, dare we ask, are the enemy? Well – the *ugly* sisters!

Am I Worth Loving?

How do we decide whether we are acceptable and have worth? The answer is that we perceive this from outside ourselves – from others – especially from those we love and respect. What makes life particularly hard is that so often when our self-esteem is at its most vulnerable, our peers are at their most hurtful. What do they sing to us on our special day when we are eight years old?

> *Happy Birthday to you.*
> *You belong in a zoo.*
> *Your face is like a monkey's.*
> *Happy Birthday to you.*

I doubt we'll ever be able to do much to change the cruelty of the very young, but life should be different around our parents. I am saddened when I hear parents make derogatory comments, even in a humorous vein, about the physical appearance of their children – especially in front of others.

The other day, Dianne complimented a teenager on her new outfit; she smiled but her mother poked a finger at a tummy that was protruding and said, 'It'll look even better when she does something about that.' Of course a parent will want to help a child who is seriously overweight, or counsel a teenager about what he or she can do about that zit on the end of their nose, but somehow we have to let our kids know that we love them anyway. That involves us being manifestly proud of them when they are at their gawkiest, most awkward, and especially if their particular features don't happen to fit what society at present calls 'attractive'. It is so hard for us to get out of the mould. The other day there was a picture in a newspaper of a young girl who had tragically lost her life. I heard a mum standing next to me say, 'Isn't it tragic – and she was so pretty.' I understand what she meant. But it wasn't any more tragic because she was pretty. It was just tragic.

The truth is that the matter of acceptance is not just relevant to the child who does not seem very physically attractive. It is probably even more important for the child who seems the epitome of all that society calls beautiful. This girl will go through her life always wondering whether her friends, employers, and the men who say they love her, actually just want her for her looks. That child, as well as her plainer friend, desperately needs to know that her mother and father love her for who she is. It will not only enrich her childhood, but it will come in handy for that day some years down the road when she asks the question of the mirror and it says, 'Sorry, honey – not you.'

But what of the other issue by which children decide whether or not their mother really does accept them?

'I Accept You Irrespective of What You Achieve'

The second way that we show our children whether or not they are accepted is by our attitude to their achievements.

One of the most testing aspects of parenthood is to balance motivating our children to reach their potential without instilling in them the belief that our love for them is conditional on how they perform. As I write, it is halfway through the month of August. For the vast majority of parents this time of year holds no special terrors, but if your child is sixteen or eighteen, the onset of the end of the summer contains trauma unimaginable: it is time for GCSE and A-level results.

Dianne and I have long since given up trying to prophesy the results of our children's examinations; in any event it is so much harder with Lloyd. When Katie came home from an examination we used to ask her how she had done. She would produce the question paper and meticulously take us through each section recalling the way she had answered, and occasionally confessing where she had been stumped. So when Lloyd hit exams we tried the same technique. He came home and we said, 'How did Maths go, son?' He answered, 'Fine'. This was very encouraging. 'Did you bring the paper home so we could look at it?' 'No – I lost it on the bus.' The next day came and with it another examination. At four o'clock we found ourselves asking, 'How was Geography?' The oracle again replied, 'Fine'. And again the paper had disappeared, this time apparently having been set fire to immediately on leaving the school. We asked about all ten subjects and received the adjudication 'Fine' to each one. Every parent wants to think the best of their children and so Dianne and I spent a blissful two weeks rejoicing that although Lloyd did not seem to have overtaxed himself on revision, his natural flair had obviously come to his aid.

It was not until we saw his school report, which had apparently only narrowly missed the same fate as befell the geography paper, that we both realised that the comment 'Fine' bore no relation at all to the results achieved. Lloyd had shown a degree of impartiality that would have done credit to an Old Bailey judge. The few successes and the cluster of disappointments had all received the same . . . 'Fine'.

Of course, since then, we have had the opportunity of observing him after many examinations and now understand that when he said 'Fine' it was actually not in relation to anything at all, least of all the recent test. It was rather a word that, loosely interpreted, meant, 'Here is a little something to keep you quiet until the truth gets out.'

I will never forget our going with Lloyd to get his GCSE results. We watched this young man walk across the playground and into the school as we sat in the car and waited. Dianne was, by now, crying but she wasn't sure why. And suddenly he appeared, results in hand. The comment that came next from his lips seemed strangely unfitting as he was now the proud possessor of a cluster of GCSEs, including English Language – 'I done wicked good, Mum!'

I promise you we have tried hard to motivate our children, and who knows whether we've succeeded or not. I am sure that we have got lots wrong in this whole area; it's possible to be too easy-going and not push a child hard enough, or to push too hard and pressurise them. But above all I have craved for them to understand that even in the middle of all the yelling, the blackmail and the forced study guides for breakfast, they should know for a certainty they were loved – anyway.

The pressure for our kids to achieve can begin at a very young age. This is how one young mum put it:

I really enjoy the 'Mother and Toddler' group; it's great for company and a chance to get out of the house, but sometimes I find it a pressure.

The mums are all very friendly but there seems to be a constant comparison of what progress our babies have made. It leaves me feeling inadequate if 'everyone else's baby' can sit up without leaning on the settee, or has started to crawl, or has quite clearly said 'Mummy'. Sometimes, though, my baby is the one in front, with most of the others lagging behind, and I feel proud at the achievement.

Already the other mothers are talking about the best nurseries – and even the best schools. I haven't thought that far ahead, but of course, I realise I must – otherwise all the other children will be reaching heights far above Gemma. There is a baby music and movement group starting up – I must get her name down straight away. And I must keep my ears open for any other classes that would aid Gemma's development. It doesn't do to fall behind in this world, and it's never too soon to begin.

I remember calling on a mum who had a six-month-old boy. I rang the bell and she yelled, 'Come in, the door's open.' I entered the hall, and hearing some noises coming from the kitchen, made my way there. I will never forget the sight that greeted me. Pamela was kneeling on the floor in front of Toby holding a knife about two inches from his face. She didn't turn round to greet me, just shouted over her shoulder, 'Grab a chair – I'll be with you in a moment.' I sat. She now turned her full attention back to the child, 'Toby, this is a knife – a *knife* Toby – this is a *knife*.' The child looked slightly more nonplussed than I and seemed more interested in the cat who at this time was tucking into Toby's stewed prune on the kitchen surface.

Eventually the knife was put down, and we had 'Toby, a *fork* – Toby, a *fork*'. I could see that this mother was utterly committed to working her way through a whole canteen of cutlery and said, 'Look – I'll come back later.' 'No,' she said, 'we're just about finished – it's his "learn a word" hour.'

I know it's not always wise to speak your mind in such moments but I couldn't resist it. 'What will he do with the word if he learns it? The child can't talk yet.' She gave me a sympathetic look and said, 'Subconscious'. I wasn't sure if she was referring to some educational principle or the look on my face, but she went on, 'It all goes into their little minds and later it will come popping out.'

Fortunately for him, Toby had a more realistic view of life than Pamela and seemed to feel no pressure at all to pop anything out apart from the normal. And it was good for him that he didn't, because in a world where achievement is everything, we can pressurise our kids to succeed and, in the process, all but rob them of their childhood.

At home I have a favourite mug; on it is a picture of a harassed mum in one of those 'family mover' vehicles which looks like a small bus. She is talking to a solitary young figure sitting next to her: 'If Simon's in Cubs, and Helen's in Brownies, and Mark's in Kung-fu, and Becky's at swimming . . . who the heck are you?'

Of course it's good to give children opportunities, and activities like piano lessons and ballet can be wonderful, so long as we don't try to put old heads on young shoulders and, in so doing, make it hard for those kids just to have fun. And when they do these things we need to lighten up a bit. The main aim should be that our kids enjoy playing the piano, learn to love ballet, not end up at the Festival Hall or starring in 'Swan Lake' in Moscow.

Sometimes we try to compensate for what we perceive to be our own failure through our children. We want them to do better than we did; we are anxious for them to have the opportunities that we missed. There's nothing wrong with any of that as long as we don't get too screwed up about it. Children quickly sense when something is important to us and they generally want to please, but not every child can win the school races, and even if they manage to, it's an awful burden to believe they've got to go on doing it. I was once attacked by an irate father who insisted that his son had beaten Lloyd in a swimming race by a millisecond. If it had been the Atlanta Olympics I might have got excited, but we were on holiday in Cornwall and it was the small hotel's *Fun* Day.

Just recently, I watched an American television programme. It was a documentary about beauty queens, except these were nine- and ten-year-olds. Mothers fussed and primped these prima-donnas who had learnt to walk, talk and ooze sex appeal before they had started their periods. Perhaps one of them will end up as Miss World. I just hope that when they do, and are surrounded by money, success and glitter, somebody will be able to explain to them where their childhood went.

We send our children into a world that will continually judge them. They will be forced to ask themselves: 'Am I clever enough?' 'Am I good with people?' 'Am I determined/flexible/focussed/laid back . . . enough?' And, of course, 'Am I attractive enough?' Matching up to the demands of others is a wearisome business. But we do our children a wonderful service if we send them into that world with an unshakeable belief that there is at least one person who, irrespective of their grades, weight or athletic genius, loves them – *anyway*. It really is the greatest gift. Most of us, as adults, are still searching for somebody to love us like that.

Where do we find examples of such love? In my experience it is so often among those who parent children with special needs. These parents face the most difficult of circumstances and often with little help or understanding. The charity I work with runs residential weekends for those parents. Some time ago a couple attended who have a Down's syndrome child. The mother said to us, 'Our son is twenty-eight years old – in all those years this is the first evening we have ever had away on our own.' Those parents do not want anybody to romanticise the task they do; nevertheless, in the everyday challenges, in the bearing of the misunderstanding of others, and the knowledge that this is a lifelong commitment, they constantly demonstrate a love that accepts – *anyway*.

New Issues Facing Christians Today

John Stott

1984 was a landmark year not least because it saw the first edition of John Stott's classic interpretation of *Issues Facing Christians Today*. With technological and medical advances and global, social and cultural changes, Christians of the 21st century face issues today never dreamt of a decade ago. Yet are these issues so different?

At the turn of the new millennium, John Stott undertook a complete revision of this work drawing on the expertise of consultants in each field of study.

Is social involvement the concern of Christians? John Stott would answer a whole-hearted 'Yes'. *New Issues* is your opportunity to start that process.

Marshall Pickering
ISBN: 0-5510-3172-7

Price: £9.99

Complexity: Can We Think Straight?

Let us suppose we are agreed that our doctrines of God, human beings, Christ, salvation and the Church commit us inescapably to becoming socially involved – not only in social service, caring in Christ's name for the victims of oppression, but also in social action, concerned for justice and social change. To be thus strongly motivated is essential, but it is not enough. Any contribution we may hope to make will depend on our comprehension of the issues. We will be wise not to blunder unprepared into the minefield of social ethics. As I once heard the late John Mackay say when he was President of Princeton Theological Seminary, 'Commitment without reflection is fanaticism in action, though reflection without commitment is the paralysis of all action.'

We should certainly not underestimate the complexity of the issues which confront humankind today. True, every generation has felt baffled by its contemporary problems; so it is not surprising that we should feel the same way. Yet the number, scale and gravity of the questions facing us at the turn of the millennium do seem to be unprecedented, owing particularly to the scientific revolution. For example, the problem of war and peace has always troubled the Christian conscience, but the international stockpiling of nuclear weapons has greatly aggravated it. Similarly, the birth of the internet and of sophisticated information technologies have brought basic questions of identity and privacy to the fore-front of discussion. And the cloning of a sheep in Scotland and of monkeys in the United States has jolted the world into a recognition of the need for serious thinking in the still young field of bio-ethics.

Clearly individual Christians cannot make themselves authorities in all these areas, and it is also doubtful whether the Church as such should be recommending particular and detailed policies. William Temple, who has certainly been the most socially concerned Archbishop of Canterbury in the twentieth century, made much of the need to distinguish between principles and policies. Writing in 1941 of continuing poverty and malnutrition in Britain, and of 'the industrial life of the country ... disgraced by chronic unemployment', he went on: 'The Church is both entitled and obliged to condemn the society characterized by these evils; but it is not entitled in its corporate capacity to advocate specific remedies.'[1] Instead, the Church should inspire its influential members (whether politicians, civil servants, business people, trade unionists or leaders in other area of public life) to seek and apply appropriate remedies. 'In other words, the Church lays down principles; the Christian citizen applies them; and to do this he utilizes the machinery of the State.'[2] Again, 'The Church cannot say how it is to be done; but it is called to say that it must be done.'[3]

The following year, in his better known book *Christianity and the Social Order*, Temple was still emphasizing the same distinction. 'The Church is committed to the everlasting Gospel . . . it must never commit itself to an ephemeral programme of detailed action.'[4] Readers of *Temple* will know that he was very far from saying that religion and politics do not mix. His point was different, namely that 'the Church is concerned with principles and not policy'.[5] The reasons why he believed the Church as a whole should refrain from 'direct political action' by developing and advocating specific programmes could be summed up as 'integrity' (the Church lacks the necessary expertise, though some of her members may have it), 'prudence' (she may prove to be mistaken and so be discredited) and 'justice' (different Christians hold different opinions, and the Church should not side with even a majority of its members against an equally loyal minority).

Even if we agree with this clarification of roles, and concede that not all Christians are responsible for working out policies, we still have to grapple with the principles, and these are by no means always easy to formulate.

Some Christians in this situation give up in despair. 'The age-long problems such as war, economics and divorce,' they say, 'have always divided Christians. There have always been pacifists and non-pacifists, capitalists and socialists, lax and rigid attitudes to divorce. And our modern problems, being more complex, are also more divisive. Besides,' they continue, 'there's no such thing as "the Christian view" on any of these problems; there is a whole spectrum of Christian views. Even the Bible does not always help us; it was written in such ancient cultures that it does not speak to our modern problems. So let us leave it to the experts and give up hope of finding a Christian answer ourselves.' Such despair denigrates God, because it denies the usefulness of his revelation as 'a lamp to our feet and a light for our path' (Psalm 119:105). To abandon hope of having anything Christian to say may even be mental laziness in the guise of a false humility.

True humility will lead us to sit patiently under the revelation of God and to affirm by faith that he can bring us to a substantially common mind. How can we believe in the Word and Spirit of God, and deny this? What is needed is more conscientious group study in which (1) we learn to pray together (2) we listen attentively to each other's positions, and to the deep concerns which lie behind them, and (3) we help each other to discern the cultural prejudices which make us reluctant and even unable to open our minds to alternative viewpoints. This kind of discipline can be painful, but Christian integrity demands it. As a result, we shall refuse to acquiesce in superficial polarizations, for the truth is always more subtle and sophisticated than that. Instead, we shall undertake some careful mapwork, plotting (and emphasizing) areas of common ground, and clarifying residual disagreements with which we will continue perseveringly to wrestle.

If despair is one reaction to the complexity of modern ethical problems, its opposite is a naive over-simplification. Some Christians (particularly evangelical Christians, I fear) have tended to jump in head first. Either unwilling or unable to grasp the issues, we have sometimes denied that there are any. Or we have reasserted our evangelical watchword about the 'perspicuity' of Scripture (namely that its message is plain or transparent), as if this meant that there are no problems. We have then given glib answers to complex questions, and have treated the Bible as if it resembled either a slot-machine (in goes your penny, out comes your answer) or that extraordinary Victorian almanac entitled *Enquire Within*, which offered information on everything.

Certainly, the way of salvation is plain or 'perspicuous',

which is what the Reformers meant by the term. But how can we assert that Scripture contains no problems when the apostle Peter himself declared that in his brother apostle Paul's letters there were 'some things that are hard to understand' (2 Peter 3:16)? Applying God's ancient Word to the modern world is also hard. To deny this is another way of denigrating God, this time by misunderstanding the nature of his self-revelation.

Thus, we dishonour God both if we assert that there are no solutions, and if we offer slick solutions. For on the one hand he *has* revealed his will to us, and on the other he has *not* revealed it in a set of neat propositions.

A Christian Mind

There is a third, better and more Christian way to approach today's complicated questions, which is to develop a Christian mind, namely a mind which has firmly grasped the basic presuppositions of Scripture and is thoroughly informed with biblical truth. It is only such a mind which can think with Christian integrity about the problems of the contemporary world.

This proposal immediately provokes opposition, however, from those Christians who have assimilated the anti-intellectual mood of today's world. They do not want to be told to use their minds, they say. Some even declare that it is 'unspiritual' to do so. In response, we draw attention to Paul's injunction to the Corinthians: 'Stop thinking like children. In . . . your thinking be adults' (1 Corinthians 14:20). The fact is that a proper use of our minds is wonderfully beneficial. (1) It glorifies God, because he has made us rational beings in his own image and has given us in Scripture a rational revelation which he intends us to study. (2) It enriches us, because every aspect of our Christian discipleship (e.g. our worship, faith and obedience) depends for its maturing on our reflection, respectively, upon God's glory, faithfulness and will. (3) It strengthens our witness in the world, because we are called like the apostles not only to 'preach' the gospel, but also to 'defend' and 'argue' it and so 'persuade' people of its truth (e.g. Acts 17:2f.; 19:8, 2 Corinthians 5:11; Philippians 1:7).

Towards the beginning of Romans 12 Paul uses the expression 'the renewing of your mind'. He has just issued his famous appeal to his Roman readers that, in gratitude for God's mercies, they should present their bodies to him as a 'living sacrifice' and as their 'spiritual worship'. Now he goes on to explain how it is possible for God's people to serve him in the world. He sets before us an alternative. One way is to 'be conformed' to this world or 'age', to its standards (or lack of them), its values (largely materialistic) and its goals (self-centred and godless). These are the characteristics of western culture. Moreover, the prevailing culture (like the prevailing wind) is not easy to stand up against. It is easier to take the line of least resistance and bow down before it, like 'reeds swayed by the wind'. Contemporary secularism is strong and subtle; the pressures to conform are great.

Paul exhorts us, however, not to be conformed to the world, but instead to 'be transformed' by the renewing of our mind with a view to discerning God's pleasing and perfect will. Here, then, is the apostle's assumption both that Christians have or should have a renewed mind, and that our renewed mind will have a radical effect on our lives, since it will enable us to discern and approve God's will, and so transform our behaviour. The sequence is compelling. If we want to live straight, we have to think straight. If we want to think straight, we have to have renewed minds. For once our minds are renewed, we shall become preoccupied not with the way of the world, but with the will of God, which will change us.

For Christian conversion means total renewal. The Fall led to total depravity – a doctrine rejected, I suspect, only by those who misunderstand it. It has never meant that every human being is as depraved as he could possibly be, but rather that every part of our humanness, including our mind, has become distorted by the Fall. So redemption involves total renewal (meaning not that we are now as good as we could be, but that every part of us, including our mind, has been renewed). The contrast is clear. Our old outlook led to conformity to the crowd; our new outlook has led us into moral non-conformity, out of concern for the will of God. Our fallen mind followed the way of the world; our renewed mind is engrossed with the will of God, as revealed in the Word of God. Between the two lies repentance, *metanoia*, a complete change of mind or outlook.

Paul writes not only of a 'renewed mind' but also of 'the mind of Christ'. He exhorts the Philippians: 'Let this mind be in you which was also in Christ Jesus' (2:5). That is, as we study the teaching and example of Jesus, and consciously put our minds under the yoke of his authority (Matthew 11:29), we begin to think as he thought. His mind is gradually formed within us by the Holy Spirit, who is the Spirit of Christ. We see things his way, from his perspective. Our outlook becomes aligned to his. We almost dare to say what the apostle could say: 'we have the mind of Christ' (1 Corinthians 2:16).

'The renewed mind'. 'The mind of Christ'. 'A Christian perspective'. 'The Christian mind'. It was Harry

Blamires who popularized this fourth expression in his book of that title, which since its publication in 1963 has had widespread influence. By a 'Christian mind' he was referring not to a mind occupied with specifically 'religious' topics, but to a mind which could think about even the most 'secular' topics 'Christianly', that is, from a Christian perspective. It is not the mind of a schizoid Christian who 'hops in and out of his Christian mentality as the topic of conversation changes from the Bible to the day's newspaper'.[6] No, the Christian mind, he writes, is 'a mind trained, informed, equipped to handle data of secular controversy within a framework of reference which is constructed of Christian presuppositions'.[7] Blamires laments the contemporary loss of Christian thinking even among church leaders: 'The Christian mind has succumbed to the secular drift with a degree of weakness and nervelessness unmatched in Christian history.'[8] Having deplored its loss, Harry Blamires sets about canvassing its recovery. He wants to witness the rise of the kind of Christian thinker who 'challenges current prejudices . . . disturbs the complacent . . . obstructs the busy pragmatists . . . questions the very foundations of all about him, and . . . is a nuisance'.[9]

Mr Blamires then goes on to list what he sees as the six essential 'marks' of a Christian mind: (1) 'its supernatural orientation' (it looks beyond time to eternity, beyond earth to heaven and hell, and meanwhile inhabits a world fashioned, sustained and 'worried over' by God); (2) 'its awareness of evil' (original sin perverting even the noblest things into instruments of 'hungry vanity'); (3) 'its conception of truth' (the givenness of divine revelation which cannot be compromised); (4) 'its acceptance of authority' (what God has revealed requires from us 'not an egalitarian attachment, but a bending submission'); (5) 'its concern for the person' (a recognition of the value of human personality over against servitude to the machine); and (6) 'its sacramental cast' (for example, recognizing sexual love as 'one of God's most efficient instruments' for the opening of man's heart to Reality).

Dr David Gill, formerly of New College, Berkeley, in his *The Opening of the Christian Mind*, proposes an alternative cluster of six characteristics which mark the Christian mind – namely, it is (1) 'theological' (focused on God and his incarnate Word), (2) 'historical' ('informed by the past, responsibly alive in the present and thoughtful about the future'), (3) 'humanist' (deeply concerned for persons), (4) 'ethical' (submissive to God's moral standards), (5) 'truthful' (committed to God's self-revelation in nature and Scripture), and (6) 'aesthetic' (appreciative of beauty as well as truth and goodness). Thus the Christian mind's 'basic contours' relate to 'God, history, persons, ethics, truth and beauty'.[10]

Both lists of six characteristics, Harry Blamires' and David Gill's, are true and valuable. But I have personally found it yet more helpful to adopt the framework provided by Scripture as a whole. For the truly Christian mind has repented of 'proof-texting' (the notion that we can settle every doctrinal and ethical issue by quoting a single, isolated text, whereas God has given us a comprehensive revelation), and instead saturates itself in the fullness of Scripture. In particular, it has absorbed the fourfold scheme of biblical history. For the Bible divides human history into epochs, which are marked not by the rise and fall of empires, dynasties or civilizations, but by four major events. – the Creation, the Fall, the Redemption and the Consummation.

First, *the Creation*. It is absolutely foundational to the

Christian faith (and therefore to the Christian mind) that in the beginning, when time began, God made the universe out of nothing. He went on to make the planet earth, its land and seas and all their creatures. Finally, as the climax of his creative activity, he made man, male and female, in his own image. The Godlikeness of humankind emerges as the story unfolds: men and women are rational and moral beings (able to understand and respond to God's commands), responsible beings (exercising dominion over nature), social beings (with a capacity to love and be loved), and spiritual beings (finding their highest fulfilment in knowing and worshipping their Creator). Indeed, the Creator and his human creatures are depicted as walking and talking together in the garden. All this was the Godlikeness which gave Adam and Eve their unique worth and dignity.

Next, *the Fall.* They listened to Satan's lies, instead of to God's truth. In consequence of their disobedience they were driven out of the garden. No greater tragedy has befallen human beings than this, that though made by God like God and for God, they now live without God. All our human alienation, disorientation and sense of meaninglessness stem ultimately from this. In addition, our relationships with each other have become skewed. Sexual equality was upset: 'your husband . . . will rule over you' (Genesis 3:16). Pain came to haunt the threshold of motherhood. Cain's jealous hatred of his brother erupted into murder. Even nature was put out of joint. The ground was cursed because of man, the cultivation of the soil became an uphill struggle, and creative work degenerated into drudgery. Over the centuries men and women have slipped from the responsible stewardship of the environment entrusted to them, and have cut down the forests, created deserts and dustbowls, polluted rivers and seas, and fouled the atmosphere with poisons. 'Original sin' means that our inherited human nature is now twisted with a disastrous self-centredness. Evil is an ingrained, pervasive reality. Although our Godlikeness has not been destroyed, it has been seriously distorted. We no longer love God with all our being, but are hostile to him and under his just condemnation.

Thirdly, *the Redemption*. Instead of abandoning or destroying his rebellious creatures, as they deserved, God planned to redeem them. No sooner had they sinned than God promised that the woman's seed would crush the serpent's head (Genesis 3:15), which we recognize as the first prediction of the coming Saviour. God's redemptive purpose began to take clearer shape when he called Abraham and entered into a solemn covenant with him, promising to bless both him and through his posterity all the families of the earth – another promise which we know has been fulfilled in Christ and his worldwide community. God renewed his covenant, this time with Israel, at Mount Sinai, and kept promising through the prophets that there was more, much more, to come in the days of the Messianic Kingdom. Then in the fullness of time the Messiah came. With him the new age dawned, the Kingdom of God broke in, the end began. Now today, through the death, resurrection and Spirit-gift of Jesus, God is fulfilling his promise of redemption and is remaking marred humankind, saving individuals and incorporating them into his new, reconciled community.

Fourth will come *the Consummation*. For one day, when the good news of the Kingdom has been proclaimed throughout the whole world (Matthew 24:14), Jesus Christ will appear in great magnificence. He will raise the dead, judge the world, regenerate the universe and bring

God's Kingdom to its perfection. From it all pain, decay, sin, sorrow and death will be banished, and in it God will be glorified for ever. Meanwhile, we are living in between times, between Kingdom come and Kingdom coming, between the 'now' and the 'then' of redemption, between the 'already' and the 'not yet'.

Here, then, are four events, which correspond to four realities – namely the Creation ('the good'), the Fall ('the evil'), the Redemption ('the new') and the Consummation ('the perfect'). This four-fold biblical reality enables Christians to survey the historical landscape within its proper horizons. It supplies the true perspective from which to view the unfolding process between two eternities, the vision of God working out his purpose. It gives us a framework into which to fit everything, a way of integrating our understanding, the possibility of thinking straight, even about the most complex issues.

For the four events or epochs we have been thinking about, especially when grasped in relation to one another, teach major truths about God, human beings and society which give direction to our Christian thinking.

The Reality of God

First, the reality of God. The fourfold biblical scheme is essentially God-centred; its four stages are disclosed from his point of view. Even the Fall, though an act of human disobedience, is presented in the context of divine commandments, sanctions and judgement. Thus, it is God who creates, judges, redeems and perfects. The initiative is his from beginning to end. In consequence, there is a cluster of popular attitudes which are fundamentally incompatible with Christian faith: e.g. the concept of blind evolutionary development, the assertion of human autonomy in art, science and education, and the declarations that history is random, life is absurd and everything is meaningless. The Christian mind comes into direct collision with these notions precisely because they are 'secular' – that is, because they leave no room for God. It insists that human beings can be defined only in relation to God, that without God they have ceased to be truly human. For we are creatures who depend on our Creator, sinners who are accountable to him and under his judgement, waifs and strays who are lost apart from his redemption.

This God-centredness is basic to the Christian mind. The Christian mind is a godly mind. More than that, it understands 'goodness' above all in terms of 'godliness'. It cannot describe as 'good' a person who is 'ungodly'. This is the clear testimony of the Bible's Wisdom Literature. The five books of Wisdom (Job, Psalms, Proverbs, Ecclesiastes and the Song of Songs) all focus, in different ways and with different emphases, on what it means to be human, and on how suffering, evil, oppression and love fit into our humanness. The Book of Ecclesiastes is best known for its pessimistic refrain, 'vanity of vanities, all is vanity', well translated by the NIV as 'meaningless, meaningless, utterly meaningless'. It demonstrates the folly and futility of a human life circumscribed by time and space. If life is restricted to the average brief lifespan, is overshadowed by pain and injustice, and culminates for everybody in the same fate, death; if it is also restricted by the dimensions of space to human experiences 'under the sun', with no ultimate reference point beyond the sun – then indeed life is as profitless as 'a chasing after wind'. Only God, Creator and Judge, Beginning and End, by adding to human life the missing dimensions of transcendence and eternity, can give it meaning, and so turn folly into wisdom.

Over against the pessimism of Ecclesiastes we read the oft-repeated maxim of the Wisdom Literature, namely, 'The fear of the Lord – that is wisdom [or its "beginning" or "principle"], and to shun evil is understanding' (Job 28:28; cf. Psalm 111:10; Proverbs 1:7, 9:10; Ecclesiastes 12:13). Here are the two major realities of human experience, God and evil. They are not equal realities, for Christians are not dualists. But they dominate life on earth. The one (God) brings human fulfilment, even ecstasy; the other (evil) human alienation, even despair. And wisdom consists in adopting a right attitude to both: loving God and hating evil, 'fearing' God with the worship which acknowledges his infinite worth, and 'shunning' evil in the holiness which despises it for its worthlessness. It is because God has made us spiritual and moral beings that religion and ethics, godliness and goodness, are fundamental to authentic humanness. Hence the tragedy of 'secularism', the closed world view which denies God and even glories in the spiritual vacuum it creates. T.S. Eliot was right to call it a 'waste land', and Theodore Roszak in *Where the Wasteland Ends* to characterize it as a desert of the spirit. 'For what science can measure is only a portion of what man can know. Our knowing reaches out to embrace the sacred.' Without transcendence 'the person shrinks'.[11] Secularism not only dethrones God; it destroys human beings.

If, because of the reality of God, the Christian mind is a godly mind, it is also a humble mind. This is another consistent theme of Scripture. When Nebuchadnezzar strutted like a peacock round the flat rooftop of his Babylonian palace claiming for himself instead of God the kingdom, the power and the glory, he went mad. Only when he acknowledged the rule of God and worshipped him, were his reason and his kingdom simultaneously restored to him. Daniel pointed out the moral: 'Those who walk in pride he is able to humble' (Daniel 4:28–37). It is a sobering story. If pride and madness go together, so do humility and sanity.

Jesus' contemporaries must have been dumbfounded when he told adults that they had to become like children if they wanted to enter God's Kingdom, and (even worse) that greatness in the Kingdom would be measured by childlike humility. We are too familiar with this teaching; it has lost its power to shock or stun. Yet Jesus not only taught it; he exhibited it. He emptied himself and humbled himself. So now, Paul adds, 'let this mind be in you which was in him'. The medieval moralists were right to see pride as the worst of the 'seven deadly sins' and as the root of the others. There is nothing so obscene as pride, nothing so attractive as humility.

Probably at no point does the Christian mind clash more violently with the secular mind than in its insistence on humility and its implacable hostility to pride. The wisdom of the world despises humility. Western culture has imbibed more than it knows of the power philosophy of Nietzsche. The world's model, like Nietzsche's, is the 'superman'; the model of Jesus remains the little child.

Thus the reality of God (as Creator, Lord, Redeemer, Father, Judge) gives to the Christian mind its first and most fundamental characteristic. Christians refuse to honour anything which dishonours God. We learn to evaluate everything in terms of the glory it gives to, or withholds from, God. That is why, to the Christian mind, wisdom is the fear of God and the pre-eminent virtue is humility.

The Paradox of Our Humanness

I turn now from God to man, from the unalloyed splendour which characterizes whatever is 'divine' to the painful ambiguity which attaches to everything 'human'. We have already seen that the biblical understanding of humankind takes equal account of the Creation and the Fall. It is this that constitutes 'the paradox of our humanness'. We human beings have both a unique dignity as creatures made in God's image and a unique depravity as sinners under his judgement. The former gives us hope; the latter places a limit on our expectations. Our Christian critique of the secular mind is that it tends to be either too naively optimistic or too negatively pessimistic in its estimates of the human condition, whereas the Christian mind, firmly rooted in biblical realism, both celebrates the glory and deplores the shame of our human being. We can behave like God in whose image we were made, only to descend to the level of the beasts. We are able to think, choose, create, love and worship, but also to refuse to think, to choose evil, to destroy, to hate, and to worship ourselves. We build churches and drop bombs. We develop intensive care units for the critically ill and use the same technology to torture political enemies who presume to disagree with us. This is 'man', a strange, bewildering paradox, dust of earth and breath of God, shame and glory. So, as the Christian mind applies itself to human life on earth, to our personal, social and political affairs, it seeks to remember what paradoxical creatures we are – noble and ignoble, rational and irrational, loving and selfish, Godlike and bestial.

Perhaps I can best illustrate this dialectic by taking two examples, first our sexuality and secondly the political process.

It is pertinent to begin with our sexuality, partly because we are all of us sexual beings, and partly because, of all the social revolutions which have taken place this century, the sexual revolution may well be the profoundest. Sexual roles (masculinity and femininity), the context for sexual intercourse (in or out of marriage), whether the traditional understandings of marriage and the family can (or even should) survive the option of homosexual partnerships, contraception, *in vitro* fertilization, artificial insemination by donor, abortion and divorce – these are some aspects of human sexuality about which radical questions are being asked today. Although the Bible gives clear instructions on some of them, we will be far better placed to grapple with individual issues if we first gain a bird's-eye view of sexuality in general by seeing it in the light of Scripture's fourfold scheme.

According to Genesis 1 and 2 God created humankind male and female in his own image from the beginning, and told them to be fruitful. Although he pronounced creation 'good', he needed to add that, 'It is not good for the man to be alone.' And he went on to ordain that the sexual complementarity of men and women was to be consummated in the mysteries of the 'one flesh' experience. Thus human sexuality, marriage, sexual intercourse and the family are all part of the creative purpose of God. Marriage (a publicly pledged, permanent, exclusive, heterosexual union) is not a human but a divine institution, which therefore in itself is not affected by changing culture. Sexual intimacy within marriage is a good gift of a good Creator.

But after the Creation came the Fall. Sin has distorted our sexuality, as it has every other human instinct, faculty and appetite. Sex has surely become a far more imperious drive than God originally intended. Unnatural sexual deviations have arisen. Although sexual love can still be enjoyed, and even wonderingly celebrated as in the Song of Songs, nevertheless it is also often spoiled by selfish demands, fears, exploitation and cruelty.

The redeeming work of Christ through his Spirit has made possible a whole new attitude to sex. This includes (in addition to a recognition of the Creator's purpose and gift) the control and sanctification of our sexual drive, a vision of self-giving love in marriage as a reflection of the relation between Christ and his Church, and a partnership between the sexes which, while not denying the responsible and caring headship which God has given to man (rooted in creation, not culture), also rejoices that in the married couple's relationship to God 'there is neither male nor female', since they are now equally justified in Christ and equally adopted into God's family (Galatians 3:26–9). At the same time, Jesus taught that for a variety of reasons some will remain single (Matthew 19:10f.; cf 1 Corinthians 7:1ff.).

What about the Consummation? In the next world after the resurrection, Jesus said, 'they will neither marry nor be given in marriage; they will be like the angels in heaven' (Mark 12:25). So, although love is eternal, marriage is not. Procreation will no longer be necessary. Relationships of love will transcend the physical, and will probably be less exclusive (though surely not less rich) than in marriage. The importance of adding this fourth stage should be clear. It contains a message both for the married (lest the union become selfish to the point even of idolatry) and for the single (that marriage is not indispensable to the attainment of full humanness).

As we try to respond Christianly to the radical sexual

challenges of today, we will find it easier to struggle with particular issues within this general biblical framework.

My second example related to 'the paradox of our humanness' concerns the political process. The nature of man (i.e. what it means to be human) has arguably been the basic political issue of the twentieth century. It has certainly been one of the chief points of conflict between Marx and Jesus, and therefore between the East and the West, namely whether human beings have any absolute value because of which they must be respected, or whether their value is only relative to the community, for the sake of which they may be exploited. More simply, are the people the servants of the institution, or is the institution the servant of the people? As John S. Whale has written, 'ideologies . . . are really anthropologies';[12] they reflect different doctrines of our humanity.

Christians should be careful not to 'baptize' any political ideology (whether of the right, the left or the centre), as if it contained a monopoly of truth and goodness. At best a political ideology and its programme are only an approximation to the will and purpose of God. The fact is that Christians are to be found in most political parties and are able to defend their membership on conscientious Christian grounds. Thus, to indulge in a blunt oversimplification, both the main political ideologies in western societies appeal to Christians for different reasons. Capitalism appeals because it encourages individual human initiative and enterprise, but also repels because it seems not to care that the weak succumb to the fierce competition it engenders. Socialism appeals, on the other hand, because it has great compassion for the poor and the weak, but also repels because it seems not to care that individual initiative and enterprise are smothered by the big government which it engenders. Each attracts because it emphasizes a truth about human beings, either the need to give free play to their creative abilities or the need to protect them from injustice. Each repels because it fails to take with equal seriousness the complementary truth. Both can be liberating. But both can also be oppressive. A wit has put this well: 'The difference between Capitalism and Socialism is that in Capitalism man exploits man, while in Socialism it's the other way round!' It is understandable that many Christians dream of a third option which overcomes the present confrontation and incorporates the best features of both.

Whatever our political colour may be, all Christians tend to advocate democracy, which was popularly defined by Abraham Lincoln as 'government of the people, by the people, for the people'. Not that it is 'perfect or all-wise', as Winston Churchill conceded in the House of Commons on 11 November 1947. 'Indeed,' he continued, 'it has been said that democracy is the worst form of government – except for all those other forms that have been tried from time to time.' The fact is that it is the wisest and safest form of government yet devised. This is because it reflects the paradox of our humanness. On the one hand, it takes the Creation seriously (that is, human dignity), because it refuses to govern human beings without their consent, and insists instead on giving them a responsible share in the decision-making process. On the other hand, it takes the Fall seriously (that is, human depravity), because it refuses to concentrate power in the hands of one person or of a few people, and insists instead on dispersing it, thus protecting human beings from their own pride and folly. Reinhold Niebuhr put it succinctly: 'Man's capacity for justice makes democracy possible; but man's inclination to injustice makes democracy necessary.'[13]

Notes

1 William Temple, *Citizen and Churchman* (Eyre & Spottiswoode, 1941), p. 82.
2 ibid. p. 83.
3 ibid. p. 84.
4 William Temple *Christianity and the Social Order* (Penguin, 1941), p. 29.
5 ibid. p. 31.
6 Harry Blamires, *The Christian Mind* (SPCK, 1963), p. 70.
7 ibid. p. 43.
8 ibid. p. 3.
9 ibid. p. 50.
10 David W. Gill, *The Opening of the Christian Mind*, 'Taking every thought captive to Christ' (Inter-Varsity Press, US, 1989), pp. 65–75 and 91. See also Arthur Holmes, *Contours of a World View* (Eerdmans, 1983) and Oliver R. Barclay, *Developing a Christian Mind* (Inter-Varsity Press, 1984).
11 Theodore Roszak, *Where the Wasteland Ends*, 'Politics and transcendence in post-industrial society' (1972; Anchor, 1973), pp. xxi and 67.
12 J.S. Whale, *Christian Doctrine* (1941; Fontana, 1957), p. 33.
13 Reinhold Niebuhr, *The Children of Light and the Children of Darkness* (Nisbet, 1945), p. vi.

The Five Love Languages

Gary Chapman

Almost one is four marriages currently end in divorce. Books abound on the subject of keeping love alive so what makes this one any different?

Gary Chapman has been a marriage counsellor for twenty years. His answer is simple as he likens expressing your love to learning a second language. The knack is working out which language of love is appropriate in your marriage.

'We may be expressing our love for one another,' says Gary, 'but the message does not come through because we are speaking what, to them, is a foreign language.'

A linguistic challenge? Which love language applies to you and your spouse?

Moody Press
ISBN: 1-8812-7315-6

Price: £9.50

2

Keeping the Love Tank Full

Love is the most important word in the English language – and the most confusing. Both secular and religious thinkers agree that love plays a central role in life. We are told that 'love is a many-splendored thing' and that 'love makes the world go round.' Thousands of books, songs, magazines, and movies are peppered with the word. Numerous philosophical and theological systems have made a prominent place for love. And the founder of the Christian faith wanted love to be the distinguishing characteristic of His followers.[1]

Psychologists have concluded that the need to feel loved is a primary human emotional need. For love, we will climb mountains, cross seas, traverse desert sands, and endure untold hardships. Without love, mountains become unclimbable, seas uncrossable, deserts unbearable, and hardships our plight in life. The Christian apostle to the Gentiles, Paul, exalted love when he indicated that all human accomplishments that are not motivated by love are, in the end, empty. He concluded that in the last scene of the human drama, only three characters will remain: 'faith, hope, and love. But the greatest of these is love.'[2]

If we can agree that the word *love* permeates human

society, both historically and in the present, we must also agree that it is a most confusing word. We use it in a thousand ways. We say, 'I love hot dogs,' and in the next breath, 'I love my mother.' We speak of loving activities: swimming, skiing, hunting. We love objects: food, cars, houses. We love animals: dogs, cats, even pet snails. We love nature: trees, grass, flowers, and weather. We love people: mother, father, son, daughter, parents, wives, husbands, friends. We even fall in love with love.

If all that is not confusing enough, we also use the word love to explain behavior. 'I did it because I love her.' That explanation is given for all kinds of actions. A man is involved in an adulterous relationship, and he calls it love. The preacher, on the other hand, calls it sin. The wife of an alcoholic picks up the pieces after her husband's latest episode. She calls it love, but the psychologist calls it codependency. The parent indulges all the child's wishes, calling it love. The family therapist would call it irresponsible parenting. What is loving behavior?

The purpose of this book is not to eliminate all confusion surrounding the word love but to focus on that kind of love that is essential to our emotional health. Child psychologists affirm that every child has certain basic emotional needs that must be met if he is to be emotionally stable. Among those emotional needs, none is more basic than the need for love and affection, the need to sense that he or she belongs and is wanted. With an adequate supply of affection, the child will likely develop into a responsible adult. Without that love, he or she will be emotionally and socially retarded.

I liked the metaphor the first time I heard it: 'Inside every child is an "emotional tank" waiting to be filled with love. When a child really feels loved, he will develop normally but when the love tank is empty, the child will misbehave. Much of the misbehavior of children is motivated by the cravings of an empty "love tank." ' I was listening to Dr. Ross Campbell, a psychiatrist who specializes in the treatment of children and adolescents.

As I listened, I thought of the hundreds of parents who had paraded the misdeeds of their children through my office. I had never visualized an empty love tank inside those children, but I had certainly seen the results of it. Their misbehavior was a misguided search for the love they did not feel. They were seeking love in all the wrong places and in all the wrong ways.

I remember Ashley, who at thirteen years of age was being treated for a sexually transmitted disease. Her parents were crushed. They are angry with Ashley. They were upset with the school, which they blamed for teaching her about sex. Why would she do this? they asked.

At the heart of mankind's existence is the desire to be intimate and to be loved by another. Marriage is designed to meet that need for intimacy and love.

In my conversation with Ashley, she told me of her parents' divorce when she was six years old. 'I thought my father left because he didn't love me,' she said. 'When my mother remarried when I was ten, I felt she now had someone to love her, but I still had no one to love me. I wanted so much to be loved. I met this boy at school. He was older than me, but he liked me. I couldn't believe it. He was kind to me, and in a while I really felt he loved me. I didn't want to have sex, but I wanted to be loved.'

Ashley's 'love tank' had been empty for many years. Her mother and stepfather had provided for her physical needs but had not realized the deep emotional struggle raging inside her. They certainly loved Ashley, and they thought that she felt their love. Not until it was almost too late did they discover that they were not speaking Ashley's primary love language.

The emotional need for love, however, is not simply a childhood phenomenon. That need follows us into adulthood and into marriage. The 'in love' experience temporarily meets that need, but it is inevitably a 'quick fix' and, as we shall learn later, has a limited and predictable life span. After we come down from the high of the 'in love' obsession, the emotional need for love resurfaces because it is fundamental to our nature. It is at the center of our emotional desires. We needed love before we 'fell in love,' and we will need it as long as we live.

The need to feel loved by one's spouse is at the heart of marital desires. A man said to me recently, 'What good is the house, the cars, the place at the beach, or any of the rest of it if your wife doesn't love you?' Do you understand what he was really saying? 'More than anything, I want to be loved by my wife.' Material things are no replacement for human, emotional love. A wife says, 'He ignores me all day long and then wants to jump in bed with me. I hate it.' She is not a wife who hates sex; she is a wife desperately pleading for emotional love.

Something in our nature cries out to be loved by another. Isolation is devastating to the human psyche. That is why solitary confinement is considered the cruelest of punishments. At the heart of mankind's existence is the desire to be intimate and to be loved by another. Marriage is designed to meet that need for intimacy and love. That is why the ancient biblical writings spoke of the husband and wife becoming 'one flesh.' That did not mean that individuals would lose their identity; it meant that they would enter into each other's lives in a deep and intimate way. The New Testament writers challenged both the husband and the wife to love each other. From Plato to Peck, writers have emphasized the importance of love in marriage.

But if love is important it is also elusive. I have listened to many married couples share their secret pain. Some came to me because the inner ache had become unbearable. Others came because they realized that their behavior patterns or the misbehavior of their spouse was destroying the marriage. Some came simply to inform me that they no longer wanted to be married. Their dreams of 'living happily ever after' had been dashed against the hard walls of reality. Again and again I have heard the words 'Our love is gone, our relationship is dead. We used to feel close, but not now. We no longer enjoy being with each other. We don't meet each other's needs.' Their stories bear testimony that adults as well as children have 'love tanks.'

Could it be that deep inside hurting couples exists an invisible 'emotional love tank' with its gauge on empty? Could the misbehavior, withdrawal, harsh words, and critical spirit occur because of that empty tank? If we could find a way to fill it, could the marriage be reborn? With a full tank would couples be able to create an emotional climate where it is possible to discuss differences and resolve conflicts? Could that tank be the key that makes marriage work?

Those questions sent me on a long journey. Along the way, I discovered the simple yet powerful insights contained in this book. The journey has taken me not only through twenty years of marriage counseling but into the hearts and minds of hundreds of couples throughout

America. From Seattle to Miami, couples have invited me into the inner chamber of their marriages, and we have talked openly. The illustrations included in this book are cut from the fabric of real life. Only names and places are changed to protect the privacy of the individuals who have spoken so freely.

I am convinced that keeping the emotional love tank full is as important to a marriage as maintaining the proper oil level is to an automobile. Running your marriage on an empty 'love tank' may cost you even more than trying to drive your car without oil. What you are about to read has the potential of saving thousands of marriages and can even enhance the emotional climate of a good marriage. Whatever the quality of your marriage now, it can always be better.

WARNING: Understanding the five love languages and learning to speak the primary love language of your spouse may radically affect his or her behavior. People behave differently when their emotional love tanks are full.

Before we examine the five love languages, however, we must address one other important but confusing phenomenon: the euphoric experience of 'falling in love.'

Notes

[1] John 13:35.
[2] 1 Corinthians 13:13.

Visit to a Second Favourite Planet

Hilary McDowell

Followers of Jesus are always 'just passing through', yet God wishes us to embrace the challenge of life on Earth to the full.

Hilary McDowell's exuberant guide to life on the 'blue planet' weaves together insights from the Bible with issues of daily concern. Her novel approach and refreshing sense of humour bring a new dimension to following the Maker's Instructions.

Discover imagined conversations with God, a look at what others have learnt, questions for group work or private meditation, and thought-provoking snippets. Intrigued?

Write yourself a memo:
Get 'on line' to the Maker's rescue plan.
Find out what the 'The Boss' wants – refer to his Book.
Watch out for the work of the 'Bad'Un'.

The Bible Reading Fellowship
ISBN: 1-8410-1144-4

Price: £5.99

From the Quartermaster's Store

Welcome Briefing

Welcome, Earthlings! So you are going to stay a while on the globe? There are a few things you need to know in order to enjoy and make the most of your time here.

First, congratulations. You have been allocated to one of the most beautiful planets created. The Maker took endless trouble over every small detail. The balance of life-sustaining elements – water, oxygen, atmosphere – even the precise angle of the tilt of the axis is positioned 'just so' in order to sustain life. He made a life-support system second to none. Please try not to upset or destroy this finely balanced mechanism or the building blocks will collapse like a row of dominoes.

Your job will be a little more difficult because the Earth has had some previous inhabitants who took all this for granted. It started with a couple called Adam and Eve. They disobeyed the Maker's instructions and bit into more than they could chew. My Boss, who is the Maker, gave them the choice, you see, because he hadn't created puppets. Unfortunately they made the wrong choice. It started a domino effect which exists even today. None of us can halt this momentum, and it still continues, but we certainly can come 'on line' to the Maker's rescue plan to save Earth's inhabitants. Speaking of which, you are one, temporarily. The other aspects of his creation – the planets, stars, plant life, animals, sea, people – all come under the domino effect. In fact, just about everything you can imagine on Earth is slowly on a downward slide away from what it was originally intended to be.

Now this in itself doesn't sound irreversible. I mean, if the will is there, and with the right tools, it is possible to imagine folk saying, 'Maybe we could all pull together and . . .' But there is one small additional problem. Well, actually it is quite a considerable problem. Come to think of it, we are talking enormous obstacle – the Enemy. He's the one who originally tricked the first human couple to disobey the Maker's instructions. Sorry to have to mention it, but he is still around, and he's mean, with a capital 'M'. The reason he is mean to Earthlings is that the Boss has no intention of letting him win the battle for Earth, but is only biding his time to let all new recruits to the planet choose whose side they want to be on before the axe falls. The Boss is fair that way.

I call the Enemy the 'Bad 'Un'. Look out for him. He is not easy to spot because he does not want to be noticed. He's an undercover sabotage agent if ever there was one.

It's better not to go searching for him. The Boss says there is no need to get jittery. But if you mean to stick around on the planet for a bit, you need to keep your eyes skinned.

Meanwhile, remember – the Boss intends you to have *life* here on the blue planet, real life, not just survival. So he is not about to abandon you. He will stick close, if you want him to. Adam and Eve weren't the only free people on the Earth. It's your choice too!

Equipment Checklist

Before advancing towards your assignment, please report to the supply store to check you are fully equipped for terrestrial habitation. You will require:

- One body in working order
- One brain in fully conscious mode
- One soul engaged in gear with the Maker

Please mark off each of these components with the official checklist and send me an order form if anything is missing. The sooner you discover a discrepancy, the better your chances for life and the quicker a deficiency can be rectified.

Body

Now, before I begin to receive a torrent of forms, I should just mention what is acceptable as regards the above three items issued. 'Working order' for a body entails that you must not be dead. It bears no relation at all to whether or not the body can fully see, hear, smell, touch, walk, jump, run or otherwise stagger around. The criterion of 'working order' owes nothing to the number of arms, legs, toes, hairs on the head or condition or prowess of the assembled parts. Please refrain from using any of the following methods to measure suitability:

- Standing in front of the mirror groaning.
- Comparison of body parts with visual images on television or in the written media, or with those of your peers who make fun of your bits, judging you inferior to their own condition.

- Listening to the lie of the Bad 'Un who attempts to hoodwink you into believing that life and value are about perfection. He likes to taunt, often saying that you will never achieve such a state with your allotted body. He is right: you won't; no one ever has. Value is not about perfection. Perfection this side of heaven is impossible. Life and value as a person are about knowing you are made in the Maker's image and he loves you. Try pursuing that to its ultimate conclusion and you will not be requisitioning me for a new body.

Regarding the frustrations of wonky bits – everything from a big nose to a serious disability or illness – it might surprise you to know that the Boss says you are allowed to talk to him about such things. Complaints will be received graciously, even though imperfections are not his fault. When logged into his two-way communication system, you will be amazed at his love and understanding. You may find yourself in receipt of a miracle, although this does not come on demand. Or he may surprise you with a novel way to cope. Or the item itself may turn out to be the kind of challenge that helps to revolutionize the world. Yes, yes, I do get a little melodramatic sometimes, but that is because my own Earth-type body issue was less than perfect. In fact, it was quite seriously 'terrestrially challenged'. As a matter of fact, there wouldn't have been an order form big enough!

I'd love to tell you what he did with it but I must not get distracted from the task in hand. It's sufficient to say that I believe that all things are possible in his strength. If he can work miracles in me, you have no problem. I would not be writing to you today as Quartermaster if he was not able to override the physical as much as any of the other imperfections of this globe.

Check your body: is it alive? Then it meets requirements for his powerful living.

Questions for Group Work or Private Meditation

What do you think of your body?

Who or what are you allowing to decide how you rate it?

Can you stand in front of your mirror and say, 'God doesn't make mistakes'?

If not, why not? Ask God what attitudes need changing.

Have you allowed God to begin working on your self-esteem?

Body-wise: list your strengths. List your imperfections. Which list is more difficult to write? Why?

Memo to yourself

Brain

The second item, a brain, must be alert. I do not refer to its intellectual capacity, its potential to be considered 'clever' by your peers, or its past record of examination success on a CV. None of these attributes is relevant to your mission on Earth. You have what you need to accomplish your given task. No tool is missing. What we are talking about here is a brain alert and free of all planetary numbing effects upon its contents.

Ask yourself: does yours have the capacity to override the terrestrial static that interferes with radio reception sometimes? A brain can become numbed to the point of obsession by every opinion upon Earth, by every idea, criticism, assessment, or even compliment gathered. At last, like the stored nuts of a squirrel, the accumulated negatives, or even false positives, take over all room inside the skull. Under such circumstances the genuine assessment of the Boss and his encouragement (or rebuke and realignment) can be blocked out. His truth needs space inside the head so that joy may come to the heart. Check your brain for alertness to what he is saying.

Please understand that this check cannot be done by any of the following methods:

- **Running away from the silence that allows you to think**. Fear of silence is a natural thing for newly initiated Earthlings. The Bad 'Un threatens boredom in the silence. He also throws all manner of pain into the memories that come swimming into focus. Yet there is great power for healing if you develop the art of inviting the Boss, and only him, into the silence. Claim victory over all negatives. Use specifically the names of God – Yahweh, or Jesus, or Holy Spirit – when chatting with him, to guard the silence from the entry of other influences. Every thought that comes pushing in to destroy your peace should be presented immediately to the Boss for healing or for further instruction.

  His Book gives great advice from him for every occasion. Check it out. In silence like this, brains are alert. Neglect the Boss's Book at your peril.

  Talk with him about what was in the silence. He's on your side, remember. The negatives and other instruction are in themselves temptations. It is important to 'take every thought captive' (2 Corinthians 10:5).

- **Attempting artificial numbing solutions to problems**. The brain is a powerful tool of communication with the Boss. At its peak of alertness, all manner of things are possible in changing and alleviating the evil, suffering and difficulties of the world. The Bad 'Un counteracts this by encouraging the use of a variety of numbing agents, which present themselves as solutions to boredom, pain and all kinds of negative feelings. Alcohol and every other drug, including the escapism of TV and computers, have all been used in this way. Many agents can be used for both good and evil. In the Boss's hands a drug, for instance, can be prescribed by a doctor to help save a life, but in the wrong hands . . . Check! Is your brain free from the control of any terrestrial element?

Are your obsessions terrestrial or eternal? Is your brain alert and attuned to the will of God? Are you linked in to the Boss's plan to revolutionize the globe? Or do you struggle to get by with an anaesthetized brain? Remember that those who barricade themselves in, meaning to hide from pain, including the emotional kind, soon lose the ability to experience joy as well.

- **Tragically deflecting your ability**. Your brain was designed and allocated for eternal purposes. It has the capacity to enhance life for many people, regardless of what you or anybody else may consider to be its intellectual capacity. But this is only possible when it is used in conjunction with the Maker's will and under the Master's instructions. The Boss can bring good by means of much that the world's systems ask you to concentrate upon. Study, exams, qualifications and practical skills are often necessary for a passage through a planetary existence, and the Boss can utilize all you might gather in these areas to enhance your ability to interact with the planet. But never forget that your mission is greater than the gathering of such requirements along the way. You are designed to spend most of your living time in somewhere other than this world. Remember that Earth is just a staging post along the way.

Questions for Group Work or Private Meditation

What most often occupies your think-time? Worries, fears, fantasies; past, present, future?

What is your present concern? What is your greatest wish?

Does any material substance numb your brain? What behaviour dulls its alertness to God?

What strategies are you using to cope with pain, suffering, failure or disappointment? Are they God-given?

How can you begin to change ineffective or sinful strategies?

Memo to yourself

Soul

Check the third piece of standard issue for Earthlings: your soul. Every human has one, whether they want it or not. Without this piece of equipment, a blue planet inhabitant would live for a short and tortured time upon a material and mortal globe, and finish. Phut! Suddenly it would just end – they call it death. The Maker designed human beings for more than this. Why do you think he designed the soul? Whatever you invest in your body and brain while you are here will get binned at death. Only what you invest in your soul will continue on. If you're not sure about this, check out his Book: you will find it full of talk of heaven, hell and eternal life. It is also full of promises on those subjects especially from Jesus. They are the best type of promises because he's been here and has seen the mess and was able to travel on before us, to somewhere else. He said he was preparing a way for us also to go. I believe him, because he is not a liar and because I know him personally. He was prepared to stake his own life on it. That took guts, and a great deal more. It took love, for us.

Before moving forward in Earth habitation, check which gear your soul is in. Please note the following warnings regarding the equipment:

- **Don't start forward with the soul in neutral**. This will not only wreck the gears but you are in danger of going nowhere. Unless, of course, you start on a steep downhill slope, in which case the entire vehicle will gain momentum and be totally out of control before you reach the bottom. On Earth, the body and mind cannot be separated from the soul. They are all one.
- **Remember to keep your brakes in proper working order**. That's what the conscience is for. Without the soul in first gear with the Boss, brakes are difficult to apply and take longer to become operative. Some Earthlings call it self-discipline. I constantly learn from the Boss that it is really about loving him enough to want to please him more than yourself.
- **Top gear is for use only when the Boss is in the driving seat**. He knows how to corner without disaster and is quite a rally driver on the sharp bends. He really ought to be at the steering wheel continuously, but life on the planet sometimes tempts us to take the wheel. Incredibly, he lets us do it. It seems he trusts us more than we trust him. Also, he wants us to get our licence by practice.

- **Highway codes must be learnt**. That's why he provided his own Book.

Is your equipment all checked? Good, now I hope you will
be able to move on to planetary living on a grand scale. The
Boss wants only the best for you, not second best, but he
doesn't deal in trendy house furnishings or updating the latest state-of-the-art gizmo. In fact, if you're hoping for life
with a capital 'L' on this planet and beyond, remember that
the 'L', in his book, stands for 'learner', not 'live it up'. He
recommends losing as much of Earth's luggage as possible. It
will only slow you down on the sprint to the finish line.

Nevertheless, feel free to requisition him at any time for
your needs. Need, not greed, is what he supplies and,
believe me, he is the best supplier in the universe. After all,
every single molecule, instinct, electrical impulse in your
make-up, every gene in the body, was designed and
moulded by him to put you together.

Exciting, isn't it? He has the technology – he *can* remake
you. Keep those order forms coming in. I like to be busy,
here in the Quartermaster's store.

Questions for Group Work or Private Meditation

Are you 'neutralizing' the soul by reserving its use for
Sundays? Or by placing it third in importance of equipment?

Have you 'unpacked' your conscience recently, or have you
consigned it to cold storage?

Who's at the wheel when you're cornering? (Check out
the Boss's Highway Code by reading his Book.)

Memo to yourself

The Relationships Revolution

Nigel D. Pollock

Sex may be the most talked about subject in contemporary western culture but it is not the key to intimacy. We want to trust people, find security and real friendships but we are afraid of being hurt.

Are we missing out on the immense privileges and blessings such relationships bring?

Nigel Pollock goes beyond trite and superficial advice to explore revolutionary ways of building relationships as we discover who and what God means us to be. Tried and tested with students, this book provides positive biblical teaching and realistic, practical help in the area of sexuality and relationships.

The challenge facing Christians is to give that help and to live out that teaching to the full.

Inter-Varsity Press
ISBN: 0-8511-1583-7

Price: £5.99

Myths Sex

3. Myths About Sex

> The great enemy of the truth is very often not the lie: deliberate, contrived and dishonest; but the myth: persistent, persuasive and unrealistic.
>
> John F. Kennedy

Sex is the most talked about and most thought about subject in contemporary western society. Alt.sex is currently Usenet's busiest newsgroup. It is read by 450,000 people worldwide, even though only about 70% of the Usenet sites carry the group. By the age of eighteen the average person will have watched nine thousand actual or suggested acts of sexual intercourse on television. I have no idea how they work these things out, but I can easily believe it.

Society's views on what is appropriate continue to shift. When I was a teenager, if there was a topless scene on television, the boys at school would be talking about it the next day. If you had not seen the programme in question you were acutely disappointed because you knew that another opportunity was not likely to arise for some time. Now, there are so many more sexually explicit scenes. Images that fuelled the adolescent fantasies of my generation now feature in adverts, as well as movies, almost on a daily basis. Any newsagent's shop presents us with an array of headlines promising to help you 'find a partner', 'enjoy bigger and better orgasms', 'experience the ultimate position'. People are desperate for advice on how to find and keep meaningful relationships.

A new group of experts has arisen to try to cope with this need. Agony aunts and uncles give popular advice in newspapers and magazines. 'Incredibly, 24% of girls would consult a magazine problem page for advice on sexual matters. That beats asking Dad, a sister/brother, boyfriend, teacher or family planning clinic'(*Sunday Mirror*/Family Planning Association). Television chat shows and discussion programmes explore issues of commitment, fulfilment and satisfaction. Some American colleges employ love coaches to give advice and help on all aspects of relationships.

The legacy of all this is that everyone is supposed to know everything about sex. We have a greater access to information than ever before. Sexual activity is an expected part of social interaction, before and outside long-term relationships.

I am glad that some of the taboos of a previous generation have been dispensed with. Many were not healthy and led to hypocrisy or oppressive legalism. List of rules without understanding became increasingly meaningless. But it is tragic that this new freedom of information and behaviour has produced such a slanted, one-sided view which has in fact given little help and promoted little choice. The liberal society can be the least tolerant of all – you are free as long as you exercise your freedom in the way expected of you.

It may well be better to have technical information about sex than the ignorance of previous generations. Educators, columnists and parents do their best to cover the basics of technique, health and safety, but people's own experience inevitably shapes their opinions about sex. This is often unacknowledged, and the advice of 'experts' may simply validate personal choices made in the past. We often lack humanity in addressing the big questions that are harder to understand. We do not know everything. We are incredibly complex beings, and relating together as men and women is a complicated business. We may well get caught in the crossfire between opinion and experience that passes for truth in society.

There is a growing body of values and ideas on what is right and wrong or acceptable in the area of sexuality. The basis of this morality, or the assumptions upon which these value judgments are based, is often difficult to discern. People frequently try to suggest that issues of sexuality and relationships can be handled without reference to biblical morality.

The morality by which most people live is not absolute. It is not to be imposed on other people. The ideas that shape our choices, expectations and lifestyle are more often rooted in popular mythology than in truth. It is worth examining some of these persistent, persuasive and unrealistic myths which have become part of the fabric of western society.

'Sex is the Most Important Thing in Life'

Sex has become a basic human right. You have the right to express your sexuality in whatever way you see fit. If you are not having sex, there is something wrong with you.

A vicar interviewed on a TV chat show said, 'If I interviewed someone who was twenty-five and still a virgin, I would think that there was something seriously wrong with them and would relate to them and counsel them on that basis.'

Sex is perceived as the key to intimacy. You do not really know somebody until you have been to bed with him or her. Yet many early encounters often take place in far from ideal circumstances, outside a context of ongoing love and commitment. One university safe-sex leaflet concluded: 'Enough of this moralizing. Sleep with whoever you want, whenever you want, but do it carefully.'

The big problem with this myth is the lack of consistency. Teenage magazines send out mixed messages. Articles on 'How to do it', with pictures of people having fun, are followed a few pages later with letters saying, 'We tried it, and we're hurting, and we need help.'

Sex is not the most important thing in life. Sexual closeness is relatively easy to achieve, but it is not the key to emotional or spiritual intimacy. Even in marriage, the idea that says 'Get the sex bit right and rest will fall into place' is the reverse of the truth.

If you did believe that sex was the most important thing in life, we would not handle it the way our society does. Anything of high value is protected, guarded and cherished. Those who reduce sex education to questions of health and safety take a minimalist view. People are more than bodies. We are minds and spirits and beings who feel. Sex and sexuality involve more than the interaction of bodies. They involve the interaction of people. You cannot put a condom on your heart or on your mind. Many people struggle with memories from the past. Others continue to feel linked with a previous partner long after the relationship has ended. Still more try to cope with a view of themselves and other people induced by sexual guilt.

'Experience is a Good Thing'

Sexual experience with a number of different partners is a positive thing. It is important to test your sexual compatibility. This is a crucial part of building commitment. You wouldn't buy a house without checking the plumbing; 'taste and try before you buy'.

Sex has become western society's initiation right. The message that comes across clearly is that everybody is doing it. 'Start using it as soon as you are 16. By 24 you will be too old' (British Rail young person's railcard ad, featuring American sex expert Dr Ruth). Sexual experience gives you status amongst your peers and confirms your standing as an adult. If you are not sexually active, you are missing out; you are not part of the in group. You do not understand what is going on.

> I'm 14 and my boyfriend is 19. I'm useless in bed as I haven't had much experience. He's had lots of girlfriends and I'm worried he compares me with them. I'd really like to please him. Can you give me some clues about how I can improve? (*Cosmopolitan*, November 1996)

The problem with this myth is that it tends to separate the physical act of intercourse from commitment and intimacy. In some cultures it is even seen as desirable for a young man to lose his virginity with the maid or a prostitute. Those who instinctively want to link sex and love would be appalled at this. But many early experiences of sex do not take place in the context of love. There is often insecurity, anxiety and a lack of mutual consideration. We can be taught from our earliest encounters that sex is about selfishness, getting what you are looking for, and achieving what you want. First experiences of anything often set the tone for the way we think about, enjoy and use it later. Sex is no different. Many people get hurt, experiencing the 'paper cup' syndrome: they feel taken up, used up, screwed up and thrown away.

Innocence is a precious thing. Virginity is something to be given away, not lost or taken.

Experience with different partners, far from enhancing commitment, often leads to the tyranny of comparison. Increasingly, we can be left searching for a composite ideal instead of appreciating a real individual.

Even in this age of safe-sex education, there is a considerable cost to sexual experience. More than 8 in every 1000 girls under the age of sixteen became pregnant in England and Wales in 1994. Over 50% of these ended in abortion. There is research that suggests a link between multiple sexual partners and infertility in later life, and between early intercourse and infertility.

'You've Got to Follow Your Feelings'

You must be true to yourself. Personal feelings are the supreme arbiter of appropriate behaviour. The question 'Is this right or wrong?' is redundant. Morality has been superseded by reality. Whatever feels good is acceptable and appropriate. Others have no right to question the decision you have made, because they cannot enter into your reality. They do not understand the force with which you feel something. Morality is a question of personal opin-

ion. 'I did it my way – how did I know it was the right way? Because it was my way and it felt right.'

The search for happiness has become the central preoccupation of our time. Following our feelings, however, does not always deliver the result we intended. Moreover, following our feelings can leave other people scattered and damaged in our wake. We are not victims of circumstance. We have the capacity to choose, to go beyond our feelings, and to evaluate the rightness of a course of action. What is presented as being true to yourself often translates as simply pleasing yourself.

Relationships are hard work. There are times when commitment takes guts, when we are required to give far more than we receive. Some marriages get into difficulty when the first child is born. Suddenly there is someone in the household who is more selfish than you are, and the marriage crumbles as the coalition of self-serving which was its foundation comes under attack. Such situations need to be worked through rather than avoided, and that process can lead to far greater satisfaction and security.

Our feelings change over time, and are affected by our emotions, circumstances and physical condition. This fluctuation makes it difficult to assess what our true feelings are. Our feelings will also be influenced by our choices and actions. Every day we choose to do things that we may not particularly feel like doing. We also choose not to do some things that we do feel like doing. This is not a betrayal of ourselves; rather, it is necessary for our well-being, and for relationships to function properly.

If, in the quest for happiness, we simply follow our feelings, we condemn ourselves to a futile search. This is especially true in relationships where two people can have feelings at the same moment which would lead them in opposite directions.

'Romantic Relationships are Personal and Private'

As long as what you do does not hurt anybody else, no-one has the right to question how you behave within a relationship. The couple has become the basic building-block of social life, and it is an unwritten rule that couples should be left to their own devices. When two people are romantically involved, a third person is one too many.

Relationships are seen to develop in quality as they become more exclusive. Couples often make significant decisions about their lives and future without reference to anyone else. The ideal is portrayed as having all your physical, emotional and spiritual needs met by one person. Consequently, when a meaningful romantic relationship develops, long-term friends are abandoned in favour of spending time with each other.

It cannot be left to individuals to determine what is right and wrong. Actions between people always have knock-on effects, which necessarily impact all our relationships and friendships. It is difficult for a couple ever to be certain that what they are doing is not damaging or hurting other people. One of the benefits of living in society, rather than being marooned on a desert island, is that we can learn from other people. We do not make moral choices in a vacuum, but in the context of responsibility and accountability to others. Most countries have laws on issues such as the age of consent, the legitimacy of sexual relationships between family members, appropriate sexual behaviour and what is permissible in the public domain and media. Most acknowledge that some restrictions on behaviour are a good thing. 'The law concerning under-age sex is not there to spoil your fun but to protect you from all kinds of damage' (*Marie Claire*, May 1997).

It is also folly to believe that all our needs can or should be met in one relationship. Romantic relationships are stronger when conducted in the context of community and family. It is not just that our bad behaviour affects other people; their good behaviour impacts us positively. We benefit from advice, support, care, help and friendship. It is unrealistic to expect one person to fulfil the role of home-maker, provider, protector, confidante, best friend, role model for the children, handyman, spiritual mentor, career advisor, financial planner and counsellor.

If we live with open hearts and open hands we shall receive much more than if we bolt the door and try to con-struct our own private utopia. The best friendships and relationships are inclusive.

'Romantic Love is the Route to Happiness and Freedom'

Only romantic love can deliver us from the drudgery of life. With-out romance, life is monochrome.

'Someday my prince will come' is the theme tune of many lives. Hours are spent looking for Mr Right, Miss Available, Mr Presentable, Miss Adequate, Mr Right Now or Miss Anybody. Weddings are still the focus of celebration and gift-giving. Some people wait for love so anxiously that they cannot get on with the rest of their lives. Lonely hearts columns feature in broadsheet and tabloid newspapers alike. People escape into novels, soaps and movies, experiencing their hopes at second hand. Others chase the shadows of what they yearn for, leafing through magazines, chatting on sex lines, or browsing the internet. Although the shadows are insubstantial, so strong is the desire for this one transforming relationship that the counterfeits quickly become addictive.

While we wait and search, we often neglect or devalue existing friendships. Focusing so strongly on the one object we do not have blurs the many other valuable aspects of your life. Focusing on the people and opportunities around us can put the missing elements in perspective.

These myths overlap and interrelate. Together they conspire to produce a set of values which dominate our approach to sex and sexuality.

On Eagles' Wings

David Adam

The saints do not seem very far away from David Adam, vicar of Lindisfarne. Fellow Northumbrian Chad was sent there in his youth to study under Aiden and his monks. From Holy Island he went out to help spread the Christian faith throughout Saxon England.

Few today can know these early Celtic saints better. David's writings on spirituality have been influential in the resurgence of interest in all things Celtic. In this story of St Chad we can learn from their seeking to make God the priority of their lives.

David writes: 'My hope is that looking at such inspiring people will help us to soar on eagles' wings, and to put our trust and hope in our God'.

Triangle
ISBN: 0-2810-5216-6

Price: £5.99

First published in 1999 by Triangle
Society for Promoting Christian Knowledge, Holy Trinity Church,
Marylebone Road, London NW1 4DU

Bishop of Mercia

In the same year that Chad was deprived of his diocese, Bishop Jaruman of Mercia died. This was the opportunity to remove Chad from the diocese of Wilfrid and for Theodore to show a friendship towards a Celtic-trained monk. Chad was obviously popular in the York area and this was not good for Bishop Wilfrid. Theodore and Wilfrid met with Wulfhere the king of Mercia and told him of the hard work and the saintly qualities of Chad. It would greatly please them if Chad could be offered the bishopric. A greater difficulty was to approach Oswy for permission to move Chad from the kingdom of Northumbria, but statesmen like Theodore and Wilfrid found a way, and Chad was appointed Bishop of Mercia. It is interesting to note that at this stage the kings had much say in church appointments and affairs.

It pleased Chad to go where his brother had worked as a missionary and where the Lindisfarne monk Diuma had been the first bishop. It made Chad think of the days gone by when Aidan was teaching and Diuma was at Lindisfarne. He would be a link with them, though he was to be the fifth Bishop of Mercia in such a short number of years.

The diocese stretched from the North Sea across to the

river Severn. The population of North Mercia was esti-
mated to be about 7,000 families, South Mercia had about
5,000 families, a further 7,000 families were in the area of
Lindsey. The base of this large diocese had been Repton. At
Repton there was a large church and a double monastery
in the Celtic style, ruled by an abbess. Chad worked from
there for a short while but longed to found his own monastery, and at a site more central to his new diocese. He
wanted a place where his own monks could both worship
and be sent out in mission. He also wanted a place that had
been hallowed by saints of old, if that were possible. On a
practical level it was also where two great roads met,
Watling Street and Ryknield Street.

At Lichfield he found a church dedicated to St Mary the
Virgin. He heard an ancient story that it was here that a
thousand Christians had died during the persecutions.
Lichfield meant the 'field of the dead'. Here ordinary men
and women had given their lives for their faith; they were
holy martyrs. Here was a place sanctified by the blood of
the saints. For a moment he remembered that Lindisfarne
had been sanctified by the blood of the Christian king
Urien ap Rheged. Here at Lichfield he would have his
monastery and base. Wherever someone has fully dedicated their life, or died for the faith, that place is special
forever.

Suddenly there was much to do. There was a protecting
wall to be raised to encircle the site. There was a cathedral
church to be built, houses for the monks, a hospice for
guests, a refectory and a place that could be used like an
island of quiet amid all the demands. The land itself had to
have the basics of life: good soil and water. Before anything
else the land had to be hallowed and claimed for the
Blessed Trinity. The monks must show to all people that

their priority was God Himself. They were called to worship and adore: 'You alone, Lord, do I seek. You alone I serve. You alone I follow.' Words came into Chad's mind from what he had learned at Rathmelsigi. We must show that we are on this earth to give glory to God.

Because it was said that on this very land Christians had died during the persecutions, the land would have to be cleansed of its past and prepared for its future. There was much to do, but it must begin with prayer. Though Chad had not been asked to consecrate a monastic site before, he knew what was required of him. He had heard Aidan speaking of forty days of prayer and fasting before any building was done. He had been told how Cedd had prepared the site at Lastingham and how his other brother Caelin had assisted. Forty days of prayer and fasting, hallowing themselves and the land, setting themselves aside as well as the earth beneath them – it was a time for consecrating themselves and the whole of the monastic site. This was a time when visions and dreams were allowed some priority. Into the forty days would be built plans and hopes for the future. Owini would find the stillness of these days difficult but it would be good for him, as he so often laboured too hard. Later he could clear the land and raise the vallum as his share in adoration. To the east of the present cathedral, Chad built his monastery on a small plot of land. Chad used a prayer similar to the one used by Aidan on Lindisfarne, and by Cedd at Lastingham. It was a prayer that looked in each direction and affirmed the presence and power of God.

God is before us
God is behind us
God's love around us,

On our right and our left.
God there above us
God there beneath us
God's might around us,
On our right and our left.
God all about us
God deep within us
God's peace be with us,
Today and forever.

Prayers like this were said over and over each day of the preparation, with the brothers joining in. Owini was allowed to mark with a spade the extent of the monastic enclosure. Chad gave each quarter his blessing. Within this enclosure would be the world in microcosm. They prayed that it would be a world renewed and restored. Within this space was an attempt at paradise regained. It was not with the foolish notion that they could keep evil out, rather with the prayer that goodness would triumph within. Here people would be able to come for peace, for healing, for renewal. The invisible walls would be a protection against violence and the power of the evil one. The gateways were meant to be gateways into the kingdom of God. Any who entered here would find mercy and protection. Crosses would be placed at the gateways as pointers to heaven and as a defence against the evil one. Some days, the prayer of dedication would be extended and acted out to emphasize that the whole site belonged to God, as does all time and space. It was not that some places did not belong to God, but through use and expectation certain places spoke more strongly than others.

Chad faced the sun as it rose and said, 'God goes before me. Into the building up of this holy place, into the future of the diocese, into the ages to come, God goes before me. There is no place I cannot meet Him, for He is there; there is no event in my life that is without His presence. The future is all unknown, but we know who goes before us and He is there to welcome and greet us. We may not know what lies ahead but we know Whom, for God goes before us.

'God is behind us, as our rearguard protecting us from attack and protecting us from the past. Places, like people, carry traces of what has been, and they can reverberate in our lives. The past needs redeeming if we are to live whole-some lives. We all carry memories and hurts that need the healing touch of our God. The land needs freeing from the violence and troubles of the past. The land, like people, needs hallowing. God's love is around us, on our right and our left. Let us and the land reveal the love of God.

'God there above us. The transcendent and holy God is above us and beyond us. We cannot contain Him by build-ing walls or churches, but we can keep Him in our hearts. The God who is above the troubles and calamities of this world, but who comes to us in the midst of them, this is the God who uplifts us, who restores us and who gives us life eternal. The God above us is the God who came down in the Word made flesh to dwell among us. God, the heaven of heavens cannot contain you, but you are willing to be held in our hearts and as you come down you lift us up.' Chad thought upon some words of St Augustine at this point.

Come, Lord Jesus, do not delay.
Come, Lord Jesus, do not tarry.
Come, Lord Jesus, draw near.
Come, Lord Jesus, come in peace.

Come as our Saviour,
Come, desire of all,
Come, show your face.
Come, and we shall be saved.
(St Augustine)

In response to this prayer, the monks were encouraged to say after each line: 'Come, Lord, come down, come in, come among us. 'Between each sentence there were long gaps as each and every one of them waited on the Lord who comes. They waited until He filled their very being. The Lord above came down and was made flesh among them.

'God there beneath us. The humble God who comes down to the lowest place, descends to hell and all the hells of our world. If we descend, He will be there also. If we fall into the dust, He is there also, and as He rises, He will rise with the dust clinging to Him, and we shall be saved. No matter how far we fall, or how often, our God is there and waiting; underneath are the everlasting arms, and the hands bear the print of the nails. All who come here will find support and hope, for we are in the very heart of God. Nothing can separate us from the love of God in Christ Jesus. Let all who are down come here, and be uplifted. Here the broken will be restored, and the weary will find new strength until they can soar like the eagle.

'God on our right and on our left. God in the height of the noonday, and in the darkness. God there in all our successes and in all our failures. God there in our joys and in our sorrows. Here let the successful rejoice, let the failures find courage, let the dextrous find joy, let the ham-fisted find encouragement. Let all, in the heights or in the depths, find God, and know his love.

The Holy Three bless us.
The Holy Three be over us.
The Holy Three be under us.
The Holy Three be all about us.
The Holy Three be within us.
And the blessing of the Three
Be upon us, evermore and evermore.
And the blessing of the Three
Be upon us, evermore and evermore.'

The area vibrated with the Presence and with peace. All of creation was dedicated to Him who created it, to Him who redeemed it, and to the Spirit who sustained it. This hallowing was not to be taken away. It was to abide forever.

After the forty days, Owini came into his own, flexing his muscles and wielding axe or mattock, using splitting wedges and hammers. Now the building began. The smells took Chad back in time to the early days on Lindisfarne; it was the smell of oak wood, soil and greenery that filled the air day after day. The smell of the soil reminded Chad of a *Gloria* he had learnt in Ireland.

The earth,
The earth rejoices in you, O God.
The earth quivers with your praise.
The earth marvels before you.
The earth magnifies your Name.
The earth praises you, its creator.
Gloria . . . Gloria . . . GLORIA.

Chad gave glory to God for all who were coming forward to serve God in the monastic life. They were joining them at such a speed that it was hard to keep the building programme going. No doubt the plague had loosened the ties of many; they needed a place to live and the knowledge that they were loved. Others came in fear of death and judgement and had to learn to look at the God who gives life and who seeks that we have life in abundance. There were soon enough in the community for Chad to long for a little island like Aidan had had off Lindisfarne, a place to escape the busyness and to be still. Even a monastery can become a place of too much action. To this end another little dwelling site was prepared, and encircled, where Chad could go with about half a dozen of his brothers. Here they would wrestle alone with God, and seek renewal and new vision. On this site, as on the main site, out of necessity there was a well. This separate place was known as a Sunderland, or *Sundorwic*, a place sundered or separated from the rest.

The king Wulfhere gave Chad and his monastery fifty hides of land in a place called Adbarvae in Lincolnshire for yet another monastery. To such places Chad travelled and he preferred to travel as always on foot. He told fellow monks that he was no more important than they were and that he was not indispensable. If he did not make it to a place, someone else would go. This did not impress Archbishop Theodore, who did not think it fitting that a bishop of the Church should be wandering around like a poor priest or a peasant. Chad should act according to his status. Chad remembered that he had twice been made deacon – a servant. Surely to be a minister is not to be elevated but to come down in the world, just as the Christ came not to be served but to serve. Theodore, as Chad's superior, forbade him to travel on foot. If he was to leave his monastic city he was to go on horseback as was fitting for a bishop. Chad said nothing but obviously his looks said something. He was not pleased, but he was under authority and he would obey. It was whilst Theodore was still with Chad that Chad was to set off on a journey. He got his walking staff as was his habit, and was about to set off when he was confronted by a very imperious-looking Theodore. This was a matter of obedience. Chad had to ride, and to emphasize the fact Theodore forcibly lifted him on to the horse, saying, 'A holy man like you needs to obey his superior. I know you are getting older, as we all are; you must not think you can walk about as when you were a boy. I command you to ride.'

It was with mixed feelings that Chad rode off. He thought back to Aidan and the time when King Oswin had given Aidan a horse with all its royal trappings, a magnificent animal and worth a fortune. Aidan had felt uncomfortable with such wealth; it played on his conscience. The solution was soon found, for Aidan met a beggar in the road and gave away the king's gift. Needless to say, the king was far from amused. What would Theodore say if Chad gave his horse away? Chad chuckled at the thought, but knew he could not do that. Still, he said out loud, 'Aidan, I hope you will forgive me.' Chad certainly got around more on horseback and had to admit it was sensible.

Back at the monastery Chad, Owini and all the brethren stopped work at the sound of the bell. Their whole lives were made up of adoration and obedience, which was symbolized in this one action. No matter what they were doing or how important they thought it, when the bell rang they stopped and went into the church to pray. This regular praying together was a strong bond between them and their God. Though Chad was away much, he prayed at the same time as his brethren and so felt he was still at one with them.

Trumbert, a student of Chad's and later to become a teacher of the Venerable Bede, noticed on more than one occasion that there was another sound that caused Chad to stop what he was doing and turn to prayer; it was the sound of a storm. Whatever Chad was involved in, whether it was reading, writing or talking to someone, if the wind was strong he stopped and prayed then and there. Often he would say to a visitor, 'Come pray with me for all travellers, all who are upon the sea, and all whose lives are in danger. Let us remember all who forget God and His power.' If the wind rose to storm force he would close his book and kneel low before the Lord, devoting himself to more prayer. If the rain grew in strength and there was thunder and lightning, Chad would leave whatever he was doing and go into the church. In the church Chad would prostrate himself before the altar and pray to the Lord. He would stay there many a long hour, reciting psalms and uttering prayers until the storm passed over. When Trumbert asked him about this, Chad replied, 'I remember terrible winds and storms on Lindisfarne. I remember ships wrecked at sea. It is the storms that remind me how frail we are and how powerful is our God.' Chad continued, 'Have you not heard it said, "The Lord also thundered in the heavens and the Highest gave out His voice. Yes, He has sent His arrows out and scattered them: He shot forth His lightning and discomforted them." Trumbert, know that it is the Lord Himself who moves the air and raises the winds, the Lord hurls the lightning flash and thunders from heaven. He seeks to rouse the people out of their sleep, that they would see His power and turn to Him. He seeks them to come to him in awe, and to remember that there is a day when the earth will burn like fire and we will all be judged. He reminds us of the day when He will scatter the proud in their conceit, when He will come on the clouds in great power. He will come to judge the living and the dead. Pray that we will be found ready and awake at His coming. For this reason I take heed of God's display of power and respond to His heavenly warning with love and fear. As often as the sky is riven and God spares us, we should give thanks to Him for His love and mercy. We should give thanks for His grace and goodness towards us. We should examine our innermost being, searching out the secrets of our hearts and purging ourselves of sin. Above all, let us behave in such a way that we do not deserve to be struck down, by adoring Him and doing His will. May the Lord find us ready for His coming. Amen.'

After two and a half years of travelling and hard work as a bishop, Chad showed signs of weakness. The brothers noticed that for a few days Chad had not been his usual self. He had not shared in the prayers, apart from in the little oratory, and had done no manual work. Chad knew that he had caught the plague, and he prayed, 'Lord, if it be your will, spare me to continue your work. If it is your will that I depart from hence, let me come to you and share with you in your kingdom.' Seven of the brethren had gone off to the church and he was left alone in the oratory. Owini was working not far away in the vegetable patch. It was February and Chad felt a chill in his bones which he knew was more than the cold of winter. The chill of death was upon him.

The Resurrection Factor

Josh McDowell

'If Jesus Christ wasn't raised from the dead, the Christian faith is worthless. But can the resurrection be proved beyond reasonable doubt?'

Widely acclaimed speaker and best selling author Josh McDowell set about answering this question. After years of extensive research into the historical evidence concerning the resurrection of Christ, Josh has found some compelling evidence. In this classic and comprehensive study, you can read for yourself what he has discovered.

If you're plagued by a sceptic's taunts, or if you have doubts of your own, this book will help to clarify your thinking. If read with an open mind, it could even transform your life.

Alpha
ISBN: 0-9465-1565-4

Special Price: £1.99

First published in the USA 1991 by
Here's Life Publishers Inc, San Bernardino, CA 92402

First British edition 1988
Revised and reprinted 1993
Reprinted 2000
Alpha is an imprint of Paternoster Publishing
PO Box 300, Carlisle, Cumbria CA3 0QS, UK

1

The Struggle

'I have had few difficulties, many friends, great successes; I have gone
from wife to wife, and from house to house, visited great countries of the
world, but I am fed up with inventing devices to fill up 24 hours of the
day.'
(Suicide Note)
Ralph Barton
Cartoonist

'I sit in my house in Buffalo and sometimes I get so lonely it's unbe-
lievable. Life has been so good to me. I've got a great wife, good kids,
money, my own health – and I'm lonely and bored . . . I often won-
dered why so many rich people commit suicide. Money sure isn't a
cure-all.'
O.J. Simpson
Football Super-Star
Millionaire
(People Magazine, June 12, 1978)

Why is it that three simple questions cast an eerie silence
across almost any university audience in America? It happens whenever I ask: 'Who are you? Why in the world are
you here? Where are you going?'

The Search Begins

As a university student, I couldn't answer those questions. Maybe you can't either. But I wanted to. Like everyone else I wanted meaning in life. I wanted to be happy. I wanted to be the happiest individual in the world. And what could be wrong with that as long as my happiness wasn't at the expense of someone else?

Happiness

Not long ago, I was riding double on a motorcycle with a friend of mine in Newport Beach, California. We were talking, laughing and having a good time. I enjoy life. In fact, it's one reason my doctor tells me I'll never get ulcers – I laugh a lot and tell people exactly what I think.

As we were riding along, two women pulled alongside us in a new Lincoln Continental. For two blocks, at 20 miles an hour, they just stared at us. Finally the lady on the passenger side rolled down her window. 'What right do you have to be so happy?' she yelled out. Before we could reply, she rolled up her window and they sped away. But the answer to her question is simple: I want to be happy and I've found the source.

Freedom

More than that I want to be free. I want to be one of the freest individuals in the world. Freedom to me is not going out and doing whatever I wish. Anyone can do that. And lots of people are. Freedom is possessing the power to do what I know I ought to do. By that definition, most people aren't free. They know what they ought to do, but they don't have the power to do it. They're in bondage. And as a university student, so was I.

Religion

I started looking for answers. Almost everyone it seems is into some sort of religion, so I took off for church. I went in the morning. I went in the afternoon. I went in the evening. But I must have found the wrong church. I felt worse inside than I did outside.

Being a practical sort of person, I chuck anything that doesn't work. So I chucked religion. The only thing I ever got out of religion was the 25 cents I put in the offering – and the 35 cents I took out for a milkshake.

But that's more than many people ever gain from 'religion', I reassured myself, and no matter what the pastor said, I still believed in God.

Prestige

I began to wonder, could prestige be the answer? Perhaps being a leader, adopting some cause, giving myself to it, and 'being known' might do it.

At the first university I attended, the student leaders held the purse strings and threw their weight around. So I ran for freshman class president and was elected.

It was neat making the decisions, spending the students' and university's money to get speakers I wanted, knowing everyone on campus, and having everyone say, 'Hi, Josh.' But, as with everything else I had tried, the glamour wore off. I would wake up Monday morning (usually with a headache from the night before), and my attitude would be, 'Well, here goes another five days.' I simply endured

Monday through Friday. Happiness revolved around three nights: Friday, Saturday and Sunday. It was a vicious circle.

Frustration

Oh, I fooled them at the university. Everyone thought I was one of the most happy-go-lucky guys around. The phrase on my political campaign button was, 'Happiness Is Josh.' I threw more parties with student money than anyone else. But my happiness was like so many other people's: It depended on my own circumstances. If things were going great, I felt great. When things would go lousy, I felt lousy.

I was like a boat in the ocean, tossed about by waves of circumstances. Everyone around me was living the same way. The faculty could tell me how to make a better living, but they couldn't tell me how to live better. Everyone could tell me what I ought to do, but none could give me the power to do it.

Frustration began to plague me.

The Struggle Continues

Few people in the universities and colleges of this country were ever more sincere than I in trying to find meaning, truth and purpose to life. Try as I might, these goals eluded me.

It was about this time I noticed a small group of people at the university – eight students and two faculty members. There was something different about their lives. They seemed to know *why* they believed what they believed.

I like to be around people like that. I don't care if people don't agree with *me*. Some of my closest friends are opposed to some things I believe. But I admire a man or woman with conviction. (Maybe that's because there are so few of them.) Contrary to most other university students, the people in this small group seemed to know where they were going.

Love Demonstrated

These people also didn't just *talk* about love. They got involved. They seemed to be riding above the circumstances of university life, when everybody else appeared to be under those circumstances. Then, too, I noticed their happiness. They appeared to possess a constant, inner source of joy. In fact, they were disgustingly happy. Obviously, they had something I didn't.

And like the average student, when somebody had something I didn't have, I wanted it. That's why you have to lock up your bicycle on the college campus. Someone may want it. If education were really the answer, the university probably would be the most morally upright community in existence. But it's not.

I wanted what I saw, so I decided to make friends with these intriguing people.

Two weeks later, we were all sitting around a table in the student union: six students and two faculty members. The conversation started to swing to God. Now, if you're insecure, and a conversation begins to centre on God, you tend to put on a big front. On every campus, in every community, in every office, there's always 'the big mouth', a person who says, 'Uh . . . Christianity, ha ha. That's for weaklings, it's not intellectual.' (Usually, the bigger the mouth, the greater the insecurity.)

The Challenge

The conversation began to bother me. Finally I looked over at one of the students, a good-looking woman (I used to think all Christians were ugly). Leaning back in my chair (I didn't want the others to think I was too interested), I said, 'Tell me, what changed your life? Why is yours so different from the other students, the leaders on this campus, the professors?'

That young woman must have had a lot of conviction. She looked me straight in the eye and, with a little smile, said two words I never thought I'd hear in a university as part of a solution.

'Jesus Christ,' she said.

'Oh, for heaven's sake, don't give me that garbage about religion,' I said.

She shot back, 'Mister, I didn't say religion; I said Jesus Christ.'

Right there she pointed out something I'd never known before. Christianity is not a religion. Religion may be defined as humans trying to work their way to God through good works. Christianity, on the other hand, is God coming to men and women through Jesus Christ, offering them a relationship with Himself.

There probably are more people with misconceptions about Christianity in universities than anywhere else in society. Recently, in a graduate seminar, I met a teaching assistant who remarked, 'Anyone who walks into a church becomes a Christian.'

'Does walking into a garage make you a car?' I replied.

There is no correlation. One becomes a Christian only by putting his trust in Christ.

My new friends challenged me intellectually to

examine the claims that Jesus Christ is God's Son; that taking on human flesh He lived among real men and women and died on the cross for the sins of mankind; that He was buried and He arose three days later and could change a person's life in the 20th century.

Intellectual Suicide

I thought it was a farce. In fact, I thought most Christians were walking idiots. I'd met some. I used to wait for a Christian to speak up in the classroom so I could beat the professor to the punch in tearing him or her up one side and down the other. I thought that if a Christian had a brain cell, it would die of loneliness. I didn't know any better.

But these people challenged me over and over. Finally, I accepted. But I did it out of pride, to refute them. I didn't know there were facts. I didn't know there was evidence a person could evaluate with his mind.

After much study and research, my mind finally came to the conclusion that Jesus Christ must have been who He claimed to be. In fact, my search to refute Christianity became the background behind my first two books. When I couldn't refute it, I ended up becoming a Christian. I now have spent thirteen years documenting why I believe that faith in Jesus Christ is intellectually feasible.

One of the crucial areas of my research to refute Christianity centred around the resurrection.

A student at the University of Uruguay said to me: 'Professor McDowell, why can't you intellectually refute Christianity?'

'For a very simple reason,' I answered. 'I am not able to explain away an event in history – the resurrection of Jesus Christ.'

After more than 1,000 hours of studying this subject and thoroughly investigating its foundation, I was forced to the conclusion that the resurrection of Jesus Christ is either one of the most wicked, heartless, vicious, hoaxes ever foisted upon the minds of men, or it is the most fantastic fact of history. It is either history's greatest delusion or the greatest miracle that history records.

The Crucial Issue

The resurrection issue removes the question, 'Is Christianity valid?' from the realm of philosophy and forces it to be an issue of history.

Does Christianity have an historically acceptable basis?

Does sufficient evidence exist to warrant belief in the resurrection?

Some of the facts relevant to the resurrection are these: Jesus of Nazareth, a Jewish prophet, claimed to be the Christ prophesied in the Jewish Scriptures. He was arrested, judged a political criminal, and crucified. Three days after His death and burial, some women went to His tomb and found the body gone. His disciples claimed that God had raised Him from the dead and that He had appeared to them various times before ascending into heaven.

From this foundation, Christianity spread throughout the Roman Empire and has continued to exert great influence down through the centuries.

Did the resurrection actually happen? Was the tomb of Jesus really empty? The controversy over these questions rages even today.

Summary

In college I was a student leader . . . in a frustrated search like everyone else for the true source of happiness and freedom. I encountered a small group of students and faculty who claimed that Jesus Christ had changed their lives. I listened only because they demonstrated the love about which they talked. As a skeptic I accepted their challenge to examine intellectually the claims that Jesus Christ was God's Son, that He was buried and arose three days later, and that He can change a person's life in the twentieth century.

Surprisingly, I couldn't refute Christianity because I couldn't explain away one crucial event in history – the resurrection of Jesus Christ. I became a believer. This book documents what I have discovered in more than one thousand hours of study on this most controversial subject.

2

Obvious Observations

'There exists no document from the ancient world witnessed by so excellent a set of textual and historical testimonies, and offering so superb an array of historical data on which the intelligent decision may be made. An honest (person) cannot dismiss a source of this kind. Skepticism regarding the historical credentials of Christianity is based upon an irrational bias.'

Clark Pinnock
Professor of Interpretations
McMasters University
Toronto

In my attempt to refute Christianity, I made nine acute observations of the resurrection that I previously had been totally unaware of.

Observation 1 – Testimony of History

Before my research on the resurrection, I had never realised there was so much positive historical, literary and legal testimony supporting its validity.

Roman History Scholar

Professor Thomas Arnold, for fourteen years the headmaster of Rugby, author of the three-volume *History of Rome*, and holder of the chair of modern history at Oxford, was well acquainted with the value of evidence in determining historical facts.

This great scholar said, 'I have been used for many years to study the histories of other times, and to examine and weigh the evidence of those who have written about them, and I know of no one fact in the history of mankind which is proved by better and fuller evidence of every sort, to the understanding of a fair inquirer, than the great sign which God hath given us that Christ died and rose again from the dead.'[1]

Textual Critic

Brooke Foss Wescott, an English scholar, said, 'Taking all the evidence together, it is not too much to say that there is no historic incident better or more variously supported than the resurrection of Christ. Nothing but the antecedent assumption that it must be false could have suggested the idea of deficiency in the proof of it.'[2]

Professor of Ancient History

Dr Paul L. Maier, professor of ancient history at Western Michigan University, concluded that, 'If all the evidence is weighed carefully and fairly, it is indeed justifiable, according to the canons of historical research, to conclude that the tomb in which Jesus was buried was actually empty on the morning of the first Easter. And no shred of evidence has yet been discovered in literary sources, epigraphy or archaeology that would disprove this statement.'[3]

Chief Justice

Lord Caldecote, Lord Chief Justice of England, has written: 'My faith began with and was grounded on what I thought was revealed in the Bible. When, particularly, I came to the New Testament, the Gospels and other writings of the men who had been friends of Jesus Christ seemed to me to make an overwhelming case, merely as a matter of strict evidence, for the fact therein stated.... The same approach to the cardinal test of the claims of Jesus Christ, namely, His resurrection, has led me as often as I have tried to examine the evidence to believe it as a fact beyond dispute.'[4]

Legal Authority

One man who was highly skilled at dealing with evidence was Dr Simon Greenleaf. He was the famous Royall Professor of Law at Harvard University and succeeded Justice Joseph Story as the Dane Professor of Law in the same university. The rise of Harvard Law School to its eminent position among the legal schools of the United States is to be ascribed to the efforts of these two men. Greenleaf produced his famous three-volume work, *A Treatise on the Law of Evidence*, which still is considered one of the greatest single authorities on this subject in the entire literature of legal procedure.

Greenleaf examined the value of the historical evidence for the resurrection of Jesus Christ to ascertain the truth. He applied the principles contained in his three-volume treatise on evidence. His findings were recorded in his book, *An Examination of the Testimony of the Four Evangelists by the Rules of Evidence Administered in the Courts of Justice.*

Greenleaf came to the conclusion that, according to the laws of legal evidence used in courts of law, there is more evidence for the historical fact of the resurrection of Jesus Christ than for just about any other event in history.

Attorney General

An Englishman, John Singleton Copley, better known as Lord Lyndhurst, is recognised as one of the greatest legal minds in British history. He was the solicitor-general of the British government, attorney-general of Great Britain, three times High Chancellor of England, and elected as High Steward of the University of Cambridge, thus holding in one lifetime the highest offices ever conferred upon a judge in Great Britain.

Upon Copley's death, among his personal papers were found his comments concerning the resurrection in the light of legal evidence and why he became a Christian: 'I know pretty well what evidence is; and I tell you, such evidence as that for the resurrection has never broken down yet.'[5]

Lord Chief Justice of England, Lord Darling, once said that 'no intelligent jury in the world could fail to bring in a verdict that the resurrection story is true.'[6]

Rationalistic Lawyer

Dr Frank Morrison, a lawyer who had been brought up in a rationalistic environment, had come to the opinion that the resurrection was nothing but a fairy-tale happy ending which spoiled the matchless story of Jesus. He felt that he owed it to himself and others to write a book that would present the truth about Jesus and dispel the mythical story of the resurrection.

Upon studying the facts, however, he, too, came to a different conclusion. The sheer weight of the evidence compelled him to conclude that Jesus actually did rise from the dead. Morrison wrote his book – but not the one he had planned. It is titled, *Who Moved the Stone?* The first chapter, very significantly is, 'The Book That Refused To Be Written.'

Literary Genius

The literary scholar, C.S. Lewis, former professor of Medieval and Renaissance literature at Cambridge University, when writing about his conversion to Christianity, indicated that he believed Christians 'to be wrong.'

The last thing Lewis wanted was to embrace Christianity. However, 'Early in 1926 the hardest boiled of all the atheists I ever knew sat in my room on the other side of the fire and remarked that the evidence for the historicity of the Gospels was really surprisingly good. "Rum thing," he went on. "All that stuff of Frazer's about the Dying God. Rum thing. It almost looks as if it had really happened once."

'To understand the shattering impact of it, you would need to know the man (who has certainly never since shown any interest in Christianity). If he, the cynic of cynics, the toughest of the toughs, were not – as I would still have put it – "safe", where could I turn? Was there then no escape?'

After evaluating the basis and evidence for Christianity, Lewis concluded that in other religions there was 'no such historical claim as in Christianity.' His knowledge of literature forced him to treat the Gospel record as a trustworthy account. I was by now too experienced in literary criticism to regard the Gospel as myth.

Finally, contrary to his strong stand against Christianity, Professor Lewis had to make an intelligent decision:

'You must picture me alone in that room in Magdalen, night after night, feeling, whenever my mind lifted even for a second from my work, the steady, unrelenting approach of Him whom I so earnestly desired not to meet. That which I greatly feared had at last come upon me. In the Trinity Term of 1929 I gave in, and admitted that God was God, and knelt and prayed: perhaps, that night, the most dejected and reluctant convert in all England.'[7]

One of my main reasons for writing *The Resurrection Factor* is to present the historical evidence that these men, and countless others like them, discovered when they were confronted with the statement that 'on the third day the tomb was empty.'

Observation 2 – Resurrection Foretold

Christ actually predicted He would rise on the third day. His claims are substantiated throughout the four Gospels. When Jesus was going up to Jerusalem, He took the Twelve Disciples aside and said to them, 'Behold, we are going up to Jerusalem. And the Son of man will be delivered to the death. They will deliver Him to the Gentiles to mock, and to scourge, and to crucify Him. And on the third day He will be raised up.'[8].

Mark points out in his Gospel that 'He began to teach

them that the Son of Man must suffer many things, and be rejected by the elders, and the chief priests, and the scribes, and be killed, and after three days rise again.'[9]

Apollyon

Tim LaHaye and Jerry B. Jenkins

The best selling 'Left Behind' series has become a thrilling testament to the book of Revelation. Over 15 million copies have been sold worldwide. The drama continues in this the fifth title in the series. As we follow the exploits of those left behind after the Rapture, the Tribulation calendar moves ever closer to the halfway point.

Written with the same gripping pace of Tom Clancy and John Grisham, *Apollyon* will fascinate and capture newcomers and fans. It's the most shocking and explicit portrayal yet as biblical prophecy is fulfilled at every turn.

Tyndale House Publishers
ISBN: 0-8423-2916-1

Special Introductory Price £7.99

Prologue

From the Conclusion of *Soul Harvest*

Rayford believed the only way to exonerate Amanda was to decode her files, but he also knew the risk. He would have to face whatever they revealed. Did he want the truth, regardless? The more he prayed about that, the more convinced he became that he must not fear the truth.

What he learned would affect how he functioned for the rest of the Tribulation. If the woman who had shared his life had fooled him, whom could he trust? If he was that bad a judge of character, what good was he to the cause? Maddening doubts filled him, but he became obsessed with knowing. Either way, lover or liar, wife or witch, he had to know.

The morning before the start of the most talked – about mass meeting in the world, Rayford approached Carpathia in his office.

'Your Excellency,' he began, swallowing any vestige of pride, 'I'm assuming you'll need Mac and me to get you to Israel tomorrow.'

'Talk to me about this, Captain Steele. They are meeting against my wishes, so I had planned not to sanction it with my presence.'

'But your promise of protection –'

'Ah, that resonated with you, did it not?'

'You know well where I stand.'

'And you also know that I tell you where to fly, not vice versa. Do you not think that if I wanted to be in Israel tomorrow I would have told you before this?'

'So, those who wonder if you are afraid of the scholar who –'

'Afraid!'

'N showed you up on the Internet and called your bluff before an international audience –'

'You are trying to bait me, Captain Steele,' Carpathia said, smiling.

'Frankly, I believe you know you will be upstaged in Israel by the two witnesses and by Dr. Ben – Judah.'

'The two witnesses? If they do not stop their black magic, the drought, and the blood, they will answer to me.'

'They say you can' t harm them until the due time.'

'I will decide the due time.'

'And yet Israel was protected from the earthquake and the meteors –'

'You believe the witnesses are responsible for that?'

'I believe God is.'

'Tell me, Captain Steele. Do you still believe that a man who has been known to raise the dead could actually be the Antichrist?'

Rayford hesitated, wishing Tsion was in the room. 'The enemy has been known to imitate miracles,' he said. 'Imagine the audience in Israel if you were to do something like that. Here are people of faith coming together for inspiration. If you are God, if you could be the Messiah, wouldn' t they be thrilled to meet you?'

Carpathia stared at Rayford, seeming to study his eyes. Rayford believed God. He had faith that regardless of his power, regardless of his intentions, Nicolae would be impotent in the face of the 144,000 witnesses who carried the seal of almighty God on their foreheads.

'If you are suggesting,' Carpathia said carefully, 'that it only makes sense that the Global Community Potentate bestow upon those guests a regal welcome sec ond to none, *you* may have a point.'

Rayford had said nothing of the sort, but Carpathia heard what he wanted to hear. 'Thank you,' Rayford said,

'Captain Steele, schedule that flight.'

One

Rayford Steele worried about Mac McCullum's silence in the cockpit of *Global Community One* during the short flight from New Babylon to Tel Aviv. 'Do we need to talk later?' Rayford said quietly. Mac put a finger to his lips and nodded.

Rayford finished communicating with New Babylon ground and air traffic control, then reached beneath his seat for the hidden reverse intercom button. It would allow him to listen in on conversations in the Condor 216's cabin between Global Community Potentate Nicolae Carpathia, Supreme Commander Leon Fortunato, and Pontifex Maximus Peter Mathews, head of Enigma Babylon One World Faith. But just before Rayford depressed the button, he felt Mac's hand on his arm. Mac shook his head.

Rayford shuddered. 'They know?' he mouthed.

Mac whispered, 'Don' t risk it until we talk.'

Rayford received the treatment he had come to expect on initial descent into Tel Aviv. The tower at David Ben Gurion cleared other planes from the area, even those that had begun landing sequences. Rayford heard anger in the voices of other pilots as they were directed into holding patterns miles from the Condor. Per protocol, no other aircraft were to be in proximity to the Condor, despite the extraordinary air traffic expected in Israel for the Meeting of the Witnesses.

'Take the landing, Mac,' Rayford said. Mac gave a puzzled glance but complied. Rayford was impressed at how the Holy Land had been spared damage from the wrath of the Lamb earthquake. Other calamities had befallen the land and the people, but to Rayford, Israel was the one place that looked normal from the air since the earthquake and the subsequent judgments.

Ben Gurion Airport was alive with traffic. The big planes had to land there, while smaller craft could put down near Jerusalem. Worried about Mac's misgivings, still Rayford couldn' t suppress a smile. Carpathia had been forced not only to allow this meeting of believers, but also to pledge his personal protection of them. Of course, he was the opposite of a man of his word, but having gone public with his assurances, he was stuck. He would have to protect even Rabbi Tsion Ben – Judah, spiritual head of the Tribulation Force.

Not long before, Dr. Ben – Judah had been forced to flee his homeland under cover of night, a universal bounty on his head. Now he was back as Carpathia's avowed enemy, leader of the 144,000 witnesses and their converts. Carpathia had used the results of the most recent Trumpet Judgments to twice postpone the Israel conference, but there was no stopping it again.

Just before touchdown, when everyone aboard should have been tightly strapped in, Rayford was surprised by a knock at the cockpit door. 'Leon,' he said, turning. 'We' re about to land.'

'Protocol, Captain!' Fortunato barked.

'What do you want?'

'Besides that you refer to me as Supreme Commander, His Excellency asks that you remain in the cockpit after landing for orders.'

'We' re not going to Jerusalem?' Rayford said. Mac stared straight ahead.

'Precisely,' Fortunato said. 'Much as we all know you want to be there.'

Rayford had been certain Carpathia's people would try to follow him to the rest of the Tribulation Force.

Fortunato left and shut the door, and Rayford said, 'I'll take it, Mac.'

Mac shifted control of the craft, and Rayford immediately exaggerated the angle of descent while depressing the reverse intercom button. He heard Carpathia and Mathews asking after Fortunato, who had clearly taken a tumble. Once the plane was parked, Fortunato burst into the cockpit.

'What was that, Officer McCullum?'

'My apologies, Commander,' Mac said. 'It was out of my hands. All due respect, sir, but you should not have been out of your seat during landing.'

'Listen up, gentlemen,' Fortunato said, kneeling between them. 'His Excellency asks that you remain in Tel Aviv, as we are not certain when he might need to return to New Babylon. We have rented you rooms near the airport. GC personnel will transport you.'

Buck Williams sat in the bowels of Teddy Kollek Stadium in Jerusalem with his pregnant wife, Chloe. He knew she was in no way healed enough from injuries she had suffered in the great earthquake to have justified the flight from the States, but she would not be dissuaded. Now she appeared weary. Her bruises and scars were fading, but

Chloe still had a severe limp, and her beauty had been turned into a strange cuteness by the unique reshaping of her cheekbone and eye socket.

'You need to help the others, Buck,'she said. 'Now go on. I'll be fine.'

'I wish you'd go back to the compound,' he said.

'I'm fine,' she insisted. 'I just need to sit awhile. I'm worried about Hattie. I said I wouldn't leave her unless she improved or became a believer, and she has done neither.'

Pregnant, Hattie Durham had been left home fighting for her life against poison in her system. Dr. Floyd Charles attended her while the rest of the Tribulation Force – including new member Ken Ritz, another pilot – had made the pilgrimage to Israel.

'Floyd will take good care of her.'

'I know. Now leave me alone awhile.'

Rayford and Mac were instructed to wait on the plane as Carpathia, Fortunato, and Mathews were received with enthusiasm on the tarmac. Fortunato stood dutifully in the background as Mathews declined to make a public statement but introduced Carpathia.

'I cannot tell you what a pleasure it is to be back in Israel,' Carpathia said with a broad smile. 'I am eager to welcome the devotees of Dr. Ben – Judah and to display the openness of the Global Community to diverse opinion and belief. I am pleased to reaffirm my guarantee of safety to the rabbi and the thousands of visitors from all over the world. I will withhold further comment, assuming I will be welcome to address the honored assemblage within the next few days.'

The dignitaries were ushered to a helicopter for the hop to Jerusalem, while their respective entourages boarded an opulent motor coach.

When Rayford and Mac finished postflight checks and finally disembarked, a Global Community Jeep delivered them to their hotel. Mac signaled Rayford not to say anything in the car or either of their rooms. In the coffee shop, Rayford finally demanded to know what was going on.

Buck wished Chloe had been able to sleep on the flight from the States. Ken Ritz had procured a Gulfstream jet, so it was the most comfortable international flight Buck had ever enjoyed. But the four of them – Ken, Buck, Chloe, and Tsion – had been too excited to rest. Tsion spent half the time on his laptop, which Ken transmitted to a satellite, keeping the rabbi in touch with his world wide flock of millions.

A vast network of house churches had sprung up – seemingly spontaneously – with converted Jews, clearly part of the 144,000 witnesses, taking leadership positions. They taught their charges daily based on the cyberspace sermons and lessons from the prolific Ben Judah. Tens of thousands of such clandestine local house churches, their very existence flying in the face of the all inclusive Enigma Babylon One World Faith, saw courageous converts added to the church every day.

Tsion had been urging the local congregations to send their leaders to the great Meeting of the Witnesses, despite warnings from the Global Community. Nicolae Carpathia had again tried to cancel the gathering at the last minute, citing thousands of deaths from contaminated water in over a third of the world. Thrilling the faithful by calling Carpathia's bluff, Tsion responded publicly on the Internet.

'Mr. Carpathia,' he had written, 'we will be in Jeru salem as scheduled, with or without your approval, per mission, or promised protection. The glory of the Lord will be our rear guard.'

Buck would need the protection almost as much as Tsion. By choosing to show up and appear in public with Ben – Juclah, Buck was sacrificing his position as Carpathia's publishing chief and his exorbitant salary. Showing his face in proximity to the rabbi's would confirm Carpathia's contention that Buck had become an active enemy of the Global Community.

Rabbi Ben – Judah himself had come up with the strategy of simply trusting God. 'Stand right beside me when we get off the plane,' he said. 'No disguises, no misdirection, no hiding. If God can protect me, he can protect you. Let us stop playing Carpathia's games.'

Buck had long been anonymously broadcasting his own cyberspace magazine, *The Truth*, which would now be his sole writing outlet. Ironically, it attracted ten times the largest reading audience he had ever enjoyed. He worried for his safety, of course, but more for Chloe's.

Tsion seemed supernaturally protected. But after this conference, the entire Tribulation Force, not to mention the 144,000 witnesses and their millions of converts, would become open archenemies of the Antichrist. Their lives would consist of half ministry, half survival. For all they had been through, it was as if the seven – year tribulation had just begun. They still had nearly five years until the glorious appearing of Christ to set up his thousand-year reign on earth.

What Tsion's Internet missives and Buck's underground electronic magazine had wrought in Israel was stunning. The whole of Israel crawled with tens of thousands of converted Jewish witnesses from the twelve tribes all over the world.

Rather than asking Ken Ritz to find an out-of-the-way airstrip where the Tribulation Force could slip

into the country unnoticed, Tsion informed his audience – and also, of course, Carpathia & Co. – of their
itinerary.

Ken had landed at the tiny Jerusalem Airport north of
the city, and well – wishers immediately besieged the plane.
A small cadre of Global Community armed guards, apparently Carpathia's idea of protection for Tsion, would have
had to open fire to get near him. The international witnesses cheered and sang and reached out to touch Tsion as
the Tribulation Force made its way to a van. The Israeli
driver carefully picked his way through the crowd and
south down the main drag toward the Holy City and the
King David Hotel.

There they had discovered that Supreme Commander
Leon Fortunato had summarily bounced their reservations
and several others' by supremely commandeering the top
floor for Nicolae Carpathia and his people. 'I assume you
have made provisions for our alternative,' Tsion told the
desk clerk after half an hour in line.

'I apologize,' the young man said, slipping Tsion an
envelope. The rabbi glanced at Buck and pulled him away
from the crowd, where they opened the note. Buck looked
back at Ken, who nodded to assure him he had the fragile
Chloe in tow.

The note was in Hebrew. 'It is from Chaim,' Tsion said.
'He writes, "Forgive my trusted friend Nicolae for this
shameful insensitivity. I have room for you and your colleagues arid insist you stay with me. Page Jacov, and you
will be taken care of."'

Jacov was Chaim Rosenzweig's driver and valet. He
loaded their stuff into a Mercedes van and soon had the
Tribulation Force installed in guest rooms at Chaim's
walled and gated estate within walking distance of the Old

City. Buck tried to get Chloe to stay and rest while he and Ken and Tsion went to the stadium.

'I didn't come here to be on the sidelines,'she said. 'I know you're concerned about me, but let me decide what I'm up to.'

At Kollek Stadium, Buck had been as stunned as the others at what had been arranged. Tsion was right. It had to have been God who used the rabbi's cyber pleas to pull together Israeli witnesses to handle the logistics of this most unlikely conference.

In spite of and in the midst of global chaos, ad hoc committees had arranged transportation, lodging, food, sound, interpretation, and programming. Buck could tell that Tsion was nearly overcome with the streamlined efficiency and no – frills program. 'All you need worry about, Dr. Ben-Judah,' he had been told, 'is being prepared to inspire and inform us when you are due at the microphone.'

Tsion smiled sadly. 'That and praying that we all remain under the care of our heavenly Father.'

'They're onto you, Rayford,' Mac said over pita bread and sauce.

Rayford shook his head. 'I haven't been a mystery to Carpathia for months. What are you talking about?'

'You've been assigned to me.'

'I'm listening.'

'I don't rate direct contact with the big man anymore. But last night I was called to a meeting with Leon. The good news is they're not onto me.'

'That *is* good. But they know about the device on the plane?'

'He didn't say, but he couldn't have been clearer that you're history. If the device still works –'

'It does.'

'N then I'll use it and keep you posted.'

'Where will I be?'

'Anywhere but here, Ray. I'm convinced the driver was listening, the car may have been bugged, the cockpit, no question about our rooms.'

'They hope I'll lead them to the others, but they'll be in plain sight in Jerusalem.'

'They want to *keep* you from the others, Ray. Why do you think we've been assigned to Tel Aviv?'

'And if I leave?'

'I'm to let them know immediately. It'll be the end of you, Ray.'

'But I've got to see my family, the rest of the Force.'

'Not here. Carpathia's pledge is to protect Tsion and the others. Not you.'

'They really think I won't go to Jerusalem?'

'They hope you will. You must not.'

Rayford sat back and pursed his lips. He would not miss the job, close as it had brought him to what was going on in the camp of the enemy. He had long wondered how the end would come to this bizarre season of his life. 'You're taking over?'

Mac nodded. 'So they tell me. There's more good news. They like and trust David.'

'Hassid? Good!'

'He's been. put in charge of purchasing. Beyond all the computer stuff he's been doing, he contracts for all major purchases. Even in avionics.'

Rayford squinted. Mac pulled a yellow sheet from his jacket and slid it across the table. 'Don't tell me he's bought me a plane,' Rayford said.

Mac snorted. 'Should have thought of that. You know those little handheld electronic organizers? David ordered a half dozen specially built. He doesn't even know yet that he won't be seeing you around anymore.'

'I can't steal these, not even from Carpathia.'

'You don't have to steal them, Ray. These are just the specs and where to get 'em. They're not cheap, but wait till you see what these babies can do. No more laptops for you guys. Well, maybe the rabbi still needs a key board, but these things are solar powered, satellite connected, and contain geographic positioning chips. You can access the Internet, send and receive, use them as phones, you name it.'

Rayford shook his head. 'I suppose he thought of tracer blocks.'

'Of course.'

Rayford stuffed the sheet into a pocket. 'What am I going to do, Mac?'

'You're going to get your tail out of this hemisphere, what else?'

'But I have to know about Arnanda. Buck will tell me only face-to-face, and he's in Jerusalem.'

Mac looked down. 'You know how that's going to go, Ray. I'd be the last one to try to tell a man about his own wife, but you know as well as I do that everything points to what you don't want to hear.'

'I haven't accepted it yet, but I have to know.'

'Buck found out for sure?'

'Sounds like it.'

'How can *he* be sure?'

'I told you about Hattie.'

'Uh-huh.'

'She knows.'

'So ask her yourself, Ray. Go home.'

'Like I wouldn't be noticed trying to slip out of here tomorrow morning.'

'The GC can't keep track of everything. Use your people's pilot – Ritz, is it? What's he got to do the next few days?'

Rayford looked at Mac with admiration. 'You're not as dumb as you look, old-timer.'

Mac pulled a phone from his pocket. 'Know his number?'

'Your phone scrambled? If I get detected talking to Ken Ritz on either of our phones–'

'You *are* dumber than *you* look if you think I'd risk that. I know the purchasing guy, remember?' Mac showed Rayford the phone, a generic model that had been doctored by David Hassid.

Rayford dialed Chloe's phone. 'Daddy!'she exulted.

'Are you here?'

Buck considered it a privilege to pray with the Israeli committee before he and Ken and Tsion headed back to find Chloe. He threw his arm around Tsion. 'Are you as tired as I am?'

'Exhausted. I only hope the Lord will allow me to sleep tonight. I am ready to share his message with these dear members of the family, and all that is left before that is to talk with Eli and Moishe. You will go with me, will you not?'

'I wouldn't miss it.'

'Me either,' Ken said.

But the news from Chloe changed Ken's plans. 'Daddy called,'she whispered. 'He needs a ride home tomorrow.'

After she explained Rayford's situation, Ken decided to get the Gulfstream out of the Jerusalem Airport and into Ben Gurion that night. Buck was nearly despondent, wanting to talk to Rayford personally. 'At least he can hear the truth about Amanda from the horse's mouth,' he said.

An hour later Jacov drove as they delivered Ken to the airport. 'We will see you back here Friday,' Tsion said, embracing him.

Chloe fell asleep on Buck's shoulder during the after – dark ride to the Temple Mount. As they left the car, the spectacular new temple gleamed on the horizon. 'I do not even want to see the new structure,' Tsion said. 'It is an abomination.'

'I can' t wait to meet the witnesses,' Chloe said.

'You may not actually meet them,' Tsion cautioned. 'These are heavenly beings with their own agenda. They may communicate with us; they may not. We approach them with great caution.'

Buck felt the usual tingle to the soles of his feet. 'You know the stories, hon.'

Chloe nodded. 'I' m not saying I' m not scared.' The three slowed as they approached the typical crowd that gathered thirty feet from the wrought – iron fence, behind which the witnesses stood, sat, or spoke. Usually they spoke. No one had seen them sleep, and none dared get closer. Threats on the lives of the two witnesses had ended in the ugly deaths of would – be assassins.

Buck's excitement masked his fatigue. He worried about Chloe but would not deny her this privilege. At the edge of the crowd of about forty, Buck was able to see past the fence to where Eli sat, Indian style, his back to the stone wall of a small building beyond the fence. His long hair and beard wafted softly in the breeze, but he was unmoving, unblinking, his leathery skin and burlaplike garb appearing to meld.

Moishe stood two feet from the fence, silent, unmoving, staring at the crowd. Occasionally someone shouted. 'Speak! Say something!' But that made others back away, obviously fearing the violent reactions they had heard of. Moishe's feet were spread, his arms loose at his sides. Earlier in the day Buck had monitored on his computer a long monologue from Moishe. Sometimes the two traded off speaking, but this day must have been all Moishe's responsibility.

'Watch them carefully,' Buck whispered to Chloe. 'Sometimes they communicate without opening their mouths. I love how everyone understands them in his own language.'

Commotion near the front caused several people to back away, opening a gap in the crowd. Someone said, 'Carpathia! It's the potentate!'

Tsion held up a hand. 'Let us stay right here,' he whispered.

Buck was riveted as Leon Fortunato smoothly super-vised GC guards who kept gawkers from Carpathia. The potentate appeared bemused, boldly moving to within ten feet of the fence. 'Hail, Potentate!' someone shouted. Carpathia half turned, holding a finger to his lips, and Fortunato nodded to a guard, who stepped toward the crowd. They backed away farther.

'Stay here,' Buck said, slipping away.

'Honey, wait!' Chloe called, but Buck moved around behind the crowd and into the shadows.

He knew he would appear to the guards as simply someone leaving. But when he was far enough away to be ignored, he doubled back through shrubbery to where he could see Carpathia's face as he stared at Moishe.

Carpathia appeared startled when Moishe suddenly spoke in a loud voice. 'Woe unto the enemy of the Most High God!'

Nicolae seemed to quickly collect himself. He smiled

and spoke softly. 'I am hardly the enemy of God,' he said. 'Many say I *am* the Most High God.'

Moishe moved for the first time, crossing his arms over his chest. Carpathia, his chin in his hand, cocked his head and studied Moishe. The ancient witness spoke softly, and Buck knew only he and Carpathia could hear him.

'A sword shall pierce your head,' Moishe said in a haunting monotone. 'And you shall surely die.'

Buck shivered, but it was clear that Carpathia was unmoved. 'Let me tell you and your companion something,' he said through clenched teeth. 'You have persecuted Israel long enough 'with the drought and the water turned to blood. You will lift your hocus – pocus or live to regret it.'

Eli rose and traded places with Moishe, beckoning Carpathia closer. The potentate hesitated and looked back to his guards, who tentatively raised their weapons. Eli spoke with such volume that the crowd dispersed and ran, and even Tsion and Chloe recoiled.

'Until the due time, you have no authority over the lampstands of God Almighty!'

The guards lowered their weapons, and Fortunato seemed to hide behind them. Carpathia's smirk remained, but Buck was convinced he was seething. 'We shall see,' he said, 'who will win in the end.'

Eli seemed to look through Carpathia. 'Who will win in the end was determined before the beginning of time. Lo, the poison you inflict on the earth shall rot you from within for eternity.'

Carpathia stepped back, still grinning. 'I warn you to stay away from the charade of the so – called saints. I have guaranteed their safety, not yours.'

Eli and Moishe spoke in unison. 'He and she who have

ears, let them hear. We are bound neither by time nor space, and those who shall benefit by our presence and testimony stand within the sound of our proclamation,'

Buck thrilled at the message and looked beyond the square to where Tsion stood with Chloe. The rabbi thrust his fists in the air as if he had gotten the message, and he walked Chloe back toward the car. Buck ducked out of the shrubs and headed around the other way, arriving in the parking lot seconds later.

'Did you hear that?' Tsion said.

Buck nodded. 'Incredible!'

'I didn't get it,' Chloe said. 'What were they saying?'

'Did it sound like Hebrew to you?' Tsion said. 'They spoke in Hebrew.'

'I heard it in English,' she said.

'Me too,' Buck said. 'They said that he *or she* who had ears to hear –'

'I heard,' Chloe said. 'I just don't understand.'

'That is the first time I ever heard them add "or she,"' Tsion said. 'That was for you, Chloe. They knew we were here. We did not have to approach them, did not have to identify ourselves, did not have to face Carpathia before we were ready. We did not even have to discuss with Eli and Moishe plans for their appearance at the stadium. They said that those who would benefit by their presence and testimony stood within the sound of their proclamation.'

'They're coming?' Chloe said. 'That is what I gather,' Tsion said. 'When?'

'At just the right time.'

Celebrate... **theWord** vouchers

£1 **off** The Sixty Minute Mother

This 'Celebrate...**the Word**' voucher £1 is redeemable against the purchase of *The Sixty Minute Mother (Hodder & Stoughton)* in all bookshops participating in the promotion. Offer valid until 30th June 2000. Voucher cannot be exchanged for cash or any other merchandise.

£4 **off** The Visitation

This 'Celebrate...**the Word**' voucher £4 is redeemable against the purchase of *The Visitation (Word)* in all bookshops participating in the promotion. Offer valid until 30th June 2000. Voucher cannot be exchanged for cash or any other merchandise.

£2 **off** The Power of a Praying Wife

This 'Celebrate...**the Word**' voucher £2 is redeemable against the purchase of *The Power of a Praying Wife (Kingsway)* in all bookshops participating in the promotion. Offer valid until 30th June 2000. Voucher cannot be exchanged for cash or any other merchandise.

£2 **off** The Bible Jesus Read

This 'Celebrate...**the Word**' voucher £2 is redeemable against the purchase of *The Bible Jesus Read (Zondervan)* in all bookshops participating in the promotion. Offer valid until 30th June 2000. Voucher cannot be exchanged for cash or any other merchandise.

£2 off New Issues Facing Christians Today

This 'Celebrate...the Word' voucher £2 is redeemable against the purchase of *The Bible Jesus Read* (Zondervan) in all bookshops participating in the promotion. Offer valid until 30th June 2000. Voucher cannot be exchanged for cash or any other merchandise.

✂

£2 off The Five Love Languages

This 'Celebrate...the Word' voucher £2 is redeemable against the purchase of *The Five Love Languages* (Moody) in all bookshops participating in the promotion. Offer valid until 30th June 2000. Voucher cannot be exchanged for cash or any other merchandise.

✂

£1 off Visit To A Second Favourite Planet

This 'Celebrate...the Word' voucher £1 is redeemable against the purchase of *Visit to a Second Favourite Planet* (BRF) in all bookshops participating in the promotion. Offer valid until 30th June 2000. Voucher cannot be exchanged for cash or any other merchandise.

✂

£1 off On Eagles' Wings

This 'Celebrate...the Word' voucher £1 is redeemable against the purchase of *On Eagles' Wings* (SPCK) in all bookshops participating in the promotion. Offer valid until 30th June 2000. Voucher cannot be exchanged for cash or any other merchandise.

✂

£2 off Relationship Revolution

This 'Celebrate...the Word' voucher £2 is redeemable against the purchase of *Relationship Revolution* (IVP) in all bookshops participating in the promotion. Offer valid until 30th June 2000. Voucher cannot be exchanged for cash or any other merchandise.

WBDVOU0

Please Complete your name & address
Title: Miss/Mr/Mrs/Ms _____
Name _____
Address _____
_____
_____
Postcode_____
email _____
Please tick here if you do not
require further mailings ☐

To the Retailer:
Please accept this voucher as a discount
payment. Vouchers will be credited less normal
discount. This voucher must be returned to:
STL Customer Services
PO Box 300
Carlisle, Cumbria, CA3 0QS
by 31 July 2000.

Name of Shop _____

STL Account No. _____

WBDVOU0

Please Complete your name & address
Title: Miss/Mr/Mrs/Ms _____
Name _____
Address _____
_____
_____
Postcode_____
email _____
Please tick here if you do not
require further mailings ☐

To the Retailer:
Please accept this voucher as a discount
payment. Vouchers will be credited less normal
discount. This voucher must be returned to:
STL Customer Services
PO Box 300
Carlisle, Cumbria, CA3 0QS
by 31 July 2000.

Name of Shop _____

STL Account No. _____

WBDVOU0

Please Complete your name & address
Title: Miss/Mr/Mrs/Ms _____
Name _____
Address _____
_____
_____
Postcode_____
email _____
Please tick here if you do not
require further mailings ☐

To the Retailer:
Please accept this voucher as a discount
payment. Vouchers will be credited less normal
discount. This voucher must be returned to:
STL Customer Services
PO Box 300
Carlisle, Cumbria, CA3 0QS
by 31 July 2000.

Name of Shop _____

STL Account No. _____

WBDVOU0

Please Complete your name & address
Title: Miss/Mr/Mrs/Ms _____
Name _____
Address _____
_____
_____
Postcode_____
email _____
Please tick here if you do not
require further mailings ☐

To the Retailer:
Please accept this voucher as a discount
payment. Vouchers will be credited less normal
discount. This voucher must be returned to:
STL Customer Services
PO Box 300
Carlisle, Cumbria, CA3 0QS
by 31 July 2000.

Name of Shop _____

STL Account No. _____

Please Complete your name & address
Title: Miss/Mr/Mrs/Ms _____
Name _____
Address _____
_____
_____
Postcode_____
email _____
Please tick here if you do not
require further mailings ☐

To the Retailer:
Please accept this voucher as a discount
payment. Vouchers will be credited less normal
discount. This voucher must be returned to:
STL Customer Services
PO Box 300
Carlisle, Cumbria, CA3 0QS
by 31 July 2000.

Name of Shop _____

STL Account No. _____

£2 off Turning Points

This 'Celebrate…the Word' voucher £2 is redeemable against the purchase of *Turning Points (OM Publishing)* in all bookshops participating in the promotion. Offer valid until 30th June 2000. Voucher cannot be exchanged for cash or any other merchandise.

✂ -

£2 off Cooking Up Worship

This 'Celebrate…the Word' voucher £2 is redeemable against the purchase of *Cooking Up Worship (Kevin Mayhew)* in all bookshops participating in the promotion. Offer valid until 30th June 2000. Voucher cannot be exchanged for cash or any other merchandise.

✂ -

£8 off New Living Translation Life Application Bible

This 'Celebrate…the Word' voucher £8 is redeemable against the purchase of *New Living Translation LAB (Tyndale)* in all bookshops participating in the promotion. Offer valid until 30th June 2000. Voucher cannot be exchanged for cash or any other merchandise.

✂ -

only £7.99 Apollyon

This 'Celebrate…the Word' title is now in paperback at a special and introductory price valid until 30th June 2000 - while stocks last. No voucher required.

- -

only £1.99 The Resurrection Factor

This 'Celebrate…the Word' title is a popular reprint at a special price valid until 30th April 2000 - while stocks last. No voucher required.

Normally £5.99

WBDVOU

Please Complete your name & address

Title: Miss/Mr/Mrs/Ms _____

Name _____

Address _____

_____

_____

Postcode_____

email _____

Please tick here if you do not
require further mailings ☐

To the Retailer:
Please accept this voucher as a discount
payment. Vouchers will be credited less norma
discount. This voucher must be returned to:
STL Customer Services
PO Box 300
Carlisle, Cumbria, CA3 0QS
by 31 July 2000.

Name of Shop _____

STL Account No. _____

WBDVOU

Please Complete your name & address

Title: Miss/Mr/Mrs/Ms _____

Name _____

Address _____

_____

_____

Postcode_____

email _____

Please tick here if you do not
require further mailings ☐

To the Retailer:
Please accept this voucher as a discount
payment. Vouchers will be credited less norma
discount. This voucher must be returned to:
STL Customer Services
PO Box 300
Carlisle, Cumbria, CA3 0QS
by 31 July 2000.

Name of Shop _____

STL Account No. _____

WBDVOU

Please Complete your name & address

Title: Miss/Mr/Mrs/Ms _____

Name _____

Address _____

_____

_____

Postcode_____

email _____

Please tick here if you do not
require further mailings ☐

To the Retailer:
Please accept this voucher as a discount
payment. Vouchers will be credited less norma
discount. This voucher must be returned to:
STL Customer Services
PO Box 300
Carlisle, Cumbria, CA3 0QS
by 31 July 2000.

Name of Shop _____

STL Account No. _____